# the PARENT'S BOOK

*Getting on well with our children*

*by*

Ivan Sokolov & Deborah Hutton

THORSONS PUBLISHING GROUP

First published 1988

© Ivan Sokolov and Deborah Hutton 1988

British Library Cataloguing in Publication Data

Sokolov, Ivan
The parents' book: getting on well with our children
1.   Children. Interpersonal relationships
with parents – For parents
I. Title    II. Hutton, Deborah
306.8'74

ISBN 0-7225-1617-7

Published by Thorsons Publishers Limited, Wellingborough,
Northamptonshire NN8 2RQ , England.

Printed in Great Britain


3   5   7   9   10   8   6   4

# CONTENTS

# INTRODUCTION

What is it, you might think, about being a parent that warrants yet another book? There are books about pregnancy and birth and looking after babies, toddlers and teenagers; books like dictionaries that allow you to look up every minor and major concern to see what you should be doing or to check whether what you are doing is good enough; books of one mother's or father's experience of their children or of being a child, and books about how other cultures have brought up their children, some relevant and some decidedly not. These books are written by a whole range of people, from professional child psychiatrists to teachers, from ordinary mums to far from ordinary dads.

So is this book any different and why might you read it? You cannot look up feeding problems in the index and find the definitive answer. Professional advice this book does not contain. Yet, within the multitude of anecdotes recounted here you will find much wisdom.

This book shares with you the experiences of some thirty to forty families who benefited from taking part in support groups that considered the day-to-day ups and downs of family life and explored ways of making the ups even more enjoyable and the downs rather rarer. They came from a mixture of cultural and educational backgrounds, and had children of all ages.

These parents all had one thing in common when they first made contact with us: they wanted to change the way they got on with their children and with each other. Very few considered that they had any 'problems' within their families, yet most wanted new choices about how to bring up their children. Some wanted little things to be different, like not getting into a battle with their toddler when he was saying 'no' to everything. Some wanted larger things to change, like the increasing gap between them and their adolescents.

Spurred on by the desire to do things differently, these parents came to a regular series of group meetings. Some came on their own, others came with their partner. Here, over the period of a school term, they shared their experiences of living with children and shouldering the responsibility for helping them grow up. They had the chance to be listened to in an atmosphere of acceptance and support so often missing in their contacts outside the group. They also had the opportunity — some for the first time — to take time to ponder on what being a parent is really all about, and how best to fulfil their role.

Discussions took place, sometimes in the whole group of eight or ten people and sometimes in pairs or groups of three. During these the participants discovered new possibilities of how to react to their children. They gained new understanding of what motivated their children to behave in sometimes unacceptable ways. Many came to appreciate how closely tied to their own experiences as children were the ways they now reacted to their offspring.

Within these groups and throughout this process they were guided and supported not by an expert but by an 'ordinary' parent, trained and experienced in a democratic style of family living. With the help and participation of this group leader, the parents learned and practised this new style. They tried it out in the support and relative safety of the group before putting it into practice at home.

Building on the success of this experience, many of these parents have kept up their contact and their regular meetings. Continuing to be supported by each other and their group leader, they have successfully gone on to adapt their approach to their children and their family lives, both in minor and sometimes major ways.

The one thing they now all have in common is aptly expressed by one of them:

*'I know that the road ahead will still be bumpy and I know that now I have a good pair of boots, the right equipment and the best possible map going!'*

This book has been written to let you share this new 'map' for bringing up children. It describes alternative ways of getting on with your children and other people that successfully tread the middle road between the authoritarian approach of many of our parents and the permissive approach that has often seemed the only other choice, however unsatisfactory.

You will meet parents in these pages who have found ways of helping children help themselves that, at the same time, relieved them of the burden of being Superparents, with cures for every physical and emotional problem. You will also meet parents who have learned to challenge their children's unacceptable behaviour and brought about changes without having to be heavy-handed and risk rebellion.

Some parents share the benefits they have gained from being prepared to put their needs first at times and not having to act as a slave to everything their children demand. They discovered that they could feel good about themselves when the tension caused by constantly caring for others was released. They have also found that when they gave something to themselves, they had far more to give when it was really needed.

These are among the ways that the parents who came to us have found of putting into practice the new ideas and understanding we shared with them.

So, what are these ideas and where did they come from? How were they developed and by whom? The group that all the contributors to this book took part in is known as Parent-Link. It has been developed by a new national voluntary organization called The Parent Network, set up by parents to support other parents in both the joys and frustrations of bringing up children.

Parent-Link had it's beginnings in my own experience as a parent, as a child and in working with other adults employed to look after children of all ages. Both personally and professionally I was unhappy with the conventional ways of relating to the younger generation. I remembered my feelings as a child of not being taken seriously by adults, of being talked down to and pushed around - 'for my own good.' I knew it had been unfair then and didn't want to repeat the pattern with my own children or those I worked with.

In my search for a different way that would allow me to develop a more open, honest and democratic relationship with young people I drew on many theoretical and practical sources: books on parent education from other parts of the world (the concept was virtually unknown in this country), courses on better communication between people, workshops on being assertive and counselling skills. Particularly influential were the ideas and practices of Carl Rogers, John Holt, Eric Fromm, Tom Gordon, Fritz Perls, Virginia Satir, Richard Bandler and John Grinder.

The experience of being a single father for nine months to sons aged four and six was perhaps the most significant part for me of this whole process of development. The break up of my marriage was a traumatic experience. The boys were both at home full-time. Sasha was not yet school age, whilst Adrian had been so unhappy at school that we were experimenting with educating him ourselves at home with the guarded agreement of the local education authorities.

We were three distraught males living on our own and it didn't feel appropriate for me always to be the strong one who looked after the emotional and physical needs of the younger two. Gradually, we found more appropriate ways of supporting each other - me putting into practice what I had learned about being democratic in the family and discovering a vast amount about their resourcefulness and potential for responsibility; they quickly learning to take into account my needs, help around the house and co-operate as part of a team.

We successfully negotiated our way around bed-times, high-quality attention for them and space alone for me. I experienced the value of encouraging them to express what they were feeling deep down inside. Above all, perhaps, I learned the importance of providing, now and again, a supportive listening ear that was, as far as possible, non-judgmental and accepting, even when the feelings concerned were directed against me.

It was certainly the confidence gained at this time that led me to start sharing what I had learned with friends and, after several years, to set up my first group for parents in London in 1984.

Since those early days, I have continued to learn from those who have come to the groups, among them the parents who have contributed to this book. I have gone on learning from my children as I am sure they have from me. I have been particularly privileged to be able to take my learnings and my inadequacies into a supportive relationship with my second wife and colleague Jacquie Pearson. Jacquie has added much to my understanding of people and relationships. In particular, she has brought a much-needed female perspective to our work.

Some four years since the first formal group, this idea of combining emotional support, education and practical skills has proved so useful and popular that Jacquie and I have set up a charitable organization training other parents to lead groups for parents in their local communities.

The Parent Network came into being in April 1986, and is training group leaders, known as Co-ordinators, in and around London, spreading now to other regions of the country. It is our intention to have groups available to all who might want them within ten years.

Along the way, Deborah Hutton has brought her great skill as a professional writer to the task of making this book a reality, spreading even further the concepts and practices that the Parent Network is all about. By the time this book is published, Deborah's new son, Archie, will doubtless be benefiting tremendously from his mother's early in-depth exposure to the principles covered here!

We hope that after reading this book you too will be inspired to explore these ideas and, if right for you, break out of the old patterns that we believe are no longer relevant for today's world. Perhaps you will consider joining a local Parent-Link group, giving yourself an opportunity to develop as second nature the new practical ways on offer. At a time when the growing rebellion of youth is, unfortunately, spawning a call for the return to Victorian family values, we believe that the small beginnings offered here can provide a workable alternative.

Like the parents in this book, we encourage you to be lenient on yourselves as you start to combine new ways of thinking and acting with the old, more conventional ways. Though we are making a call for democratic relationships within the family, we, as parents, know that there are times when it is appropriate for each of us to revert firmly to the power of the conventional role with all its responsibilities that we cannot shrug aside. My only plea is that you, like the people in this book, do so with awareness and compassion.

IVAN SOKOLOV

---

*Publisher's note*
All the quotations in this book are from parents commenting on real-life situations and experiences, but their names have been changed to protect their privacy

# CHAPTER 1

# PARENTS AND CHILDREN

'It has really changed my whole life, having children, the way I think and feel as a person. It's definitely the most important single thing that's ever happened to me ...'

There's nothing more full of promise than a brand new baby. Even before the birth we have certain expectations and hopes. As we nurture this new life, we know what sort of parents we want to be — responsible, loving, 'good' parents who play with their children, encourage and support them, let them know how special they are. We also know what sort of parents we don't want to be — the cross impatient type who constantly nag and say 'No', drag their children along by the arm, stamp on their natural expressiveness and curiosity, smack them in the supermarket.

*We did not discuss children very much before we had them — only to the extent of judging the way our friends were bringing up theirs. I remember that we were highly critical, the way we looked at other parents, judging them and heaping blame when they didn't act the way we felt they should, the way WE would.'*

*'I don't think I ever thought about it. I certainly can't remember talking with my husband in any realistic way about what type of approach we were going to adopt. It never occurred to me. I just suddenly found that I was a parent.'*

Children are conceived and helped into this world in a whole manner of ways and for a variety of reasons. Some are carefully planned, others happen almost by chance, some

are greeted with great joy whether planned for or not, others with cautious interest. Luckily for most infants, their arrival is treated as a blessing.

Looking back, parents say that the impact of children upon their lives is greater than anything before or afterwards – for good and for bad. Children have a way of bringing out both the very worst and very best of us. One mother summed up: 'My kids get down to the guts of me. I've never regarded myself as a particularly angry person. Before I had Luke, I didn't even know that I *could* get angry . . .' Along with these less-than-wonderful aspects of ourselves, however, it seems new strengths are also waiting to emerge . . . In meeting our children's needs, we find new levels of tolerance, love, commitment and ingenuity we may not have been aware of before. 'I still do things that embarrass them dreadfully, like singing in the street,' said one mother, 'but my children love me as a mother and that counts for a lot. I feel more fully human, more generous, and certainly less selfish, for having them around.'

The parents we see in the groups may share many frustrations and difficulties but they have many joys in common too – the laughter, jokes and games; the really spontaneous hugs and kisses that make family life so endlessly rewarding. 'If you give it just a tiny tiny half an inch,' said one mother, 'you get a mile back. It really does change life into a delight.'

*'When I was pregnant, all these people came out with dire warnings about how having children would change my life as though it were all going to be for the worse. Yes, my children have changed my life and I do find it more tiring than I ever imagined but it's also more rewarding, more fun, than I ever imagined too. I've never been in the slightest doubt that the change in my own life has been one for the better.'*

*'Although I have moments which defeat me nearly every day, nine days out of ten I think "aren't I lucky, here I am with my children — I've still got three of them at home — and I'm really able to enjoy them . . ." I think of Maria Montessori's words that when you're getting fed up with your children climbing into bed with you every morning you must remember that when you're sixty-seven no-one will want to climb into bed with you! It takes someone else to jerk us into those realizations. I've only got one little one that climbs into bed regularly, the others come sporadically, but it's still lovely . . .'*

*'So many people moan all the time about their children —* *about getting up early, being exhausted, the cost of shoes. I was amazed at the joy that I felt. I couldn't believe it. He was so wonderful I couldn't believe he wasn't going to be taken away again.'*

A common feeling amongst parents was expressed eloquently to us by one father who had been brought up in Europe in the traumatic war years and so missed out on the experience of childhood as most people know it. 'I suppose I am rediscovering the child in me, learning maybe even for the first time how to play, laugh, cry, love and at times hate like a child. It has to be one of the most significant features for me about being Miles' father.'

There is much about living with small children that frees us to indulge in the important simple joys of life. Babies and small children are so rewarding to cuddle; they smell good, their bodies are soft and expressive and they cuddle back! We are given the opportunity to roll around, sing (whatever we sound like!), run, climb, paint and draw, dress up, feed the ducks in the park, go to the funfair, slide and swing, get muddy and above all forget we are grown up for a while as many of us may not have done for years.

*'It's that kind of simplicity about*

*everything that I like. The adult
world seems complicated and
fraught, somehow, with all the
grown-up games you have to
play. Whilst the children just go
whoosh! and bring everything
out into the open. That's one of
the great gifts that I think
children give – straightforward-
ness.'*

For all their much-broadcasted
intransigence, parents of teenagers
find the joys remain very much in
evidence; they just shift in emphasis a little.

*'Some of her decisions I disagree
with. Others I abhor! But if I can
keep quiet about the fact that
her socks are rolled down
around her ankles when I think
they should be pulled up to her
knees and her hair is in her eyes
when I think it should be off her
forehead — if I can manage not
to fly off the handle, I can take
real pleasure in her growing
independence, watching her
work things out for herself...'*

It's one of the real delights of family
life that the seemingly endless give,
give, giving is reciprocated where
least looked for. We expect to have
a formative influence on our
children's lives and characters. It
can come as a surprise to find that
they have every bit as much of an
impact on our own lives. One
father points to the way his son's

formidable powers of observation
have opened his own eyes to the
world around him. 'I used to hate
insects but now I share their fas-
cination. Now it's "Look at this
worm and see how many lines he
has on him". It's a different way of
looking at life totally.'

Another parent found that her
children provided her with the
opportunity to slow down and shift
focus. 'I discovered the rich world
of the neighbourhood and its
inhabitants, made friends with
other families and developed supportive networks in the local community — all things which are
invisible to non-parents leaving
early and returning late ...'

Having children certainly stretches us to the limits. If we let them,
they help us to grow and develop
every bit as much as we help them.
Living with children, teenagers
especially, keeps us on our toes: by
continually challenging our ideas
and opinions, they help prevent us
slumping back into what might
otherwise be an overly complacent
view of the world.

Even the most educationally
ambitious parent, pushing her
child to 'get ahead', would admit
that the learning is not all one way:
children have as much to teach as
to be taught, providing examples
we adults would do well to follow
— whether it's living in the simple
trust that tomorrow will look after
itself or being willing to try new

ways when the old ones don't work and refusing to be put off by 'failure' in the way we adults all too often are.

*'One of my sons gets into a very powerful earthquake of anger. My own way has been never to explode. How I long to be able to get things out like he does and get them over with!'*

*'I never really knew what it meant to love unconditionally until my children taught me. My wife and I would row occasionally and I would be decidedly unloving for quite a while. But the children don't do that. However horrible I am to them, however much they express their instant displeasure with me, the very next moment their love shines through again ...'*

## What are your dreams for the future?

In the day-to-day business of bringing up children, washing, cleaning, and mending He-man figures, it is easy to lose sight of the ideals, beliefs and values that we hold. We can forget about joy, happiness, integrity and love. We all have dreams for our children. What are yours? How would you like your children to be as adults when they are out on their own? Think about it for a few minutes then write it down.

_____

_____

_____

_____

_____

_____

_____

_____

_____

_____

Just as with the joys, the pressures of parenthood may be unimaginable. The twenty-four-hour-a-day responsibility for a new individual cannot easily be prepared for in advance.

Mary Amersham, one of the mothers who attended the group, told how she came down to earth with a thump when she went home with a baby in her arms. 'Suddenly it was just us — me and this tiny baby — and it was terrifying, *so* scary. The responsibility was like a great big millstone round my neck.' It was a cruel awakening, too, to find that not only was she not the ideal mother of her imaginings, Ann was far from the ideal baby — constantly screaming and never settling.

'Within a short time I rang up the hospital and said, "Can I come back in?" and I was really quite surprised when they said no. And I said, "Where can I go? I can't cope with all this." I can remember saying, "Where's the manual? Where's the course?" I've been in computers and you are never let loose near any new machine until you have either done the course or read the manual. I remember wondering why I had been *allowed* to have a baby, when I didn't know the least thing about it.'

Mary, like many modern parents consulted books and received lots of advice, often unasked and usually conflicting, from health visitors, in-laws, family and friends about how to feed and quiet, wash and discipline her child. Eventually she realised these 'experts' couldn't help her very much. 'I discovered by the end of the week that nobody knew better — nobody out there knew more about how to take care of this baby than I did. And I didn't know anything.'

With the optimism of those who know little, most parents-to-be feel sure that love is enough; that if they are good, decent and loving to their children, accepting that they are individuals, surely they'll win through. . .

*'I didn't dream for a moment that I would have to* think *about how to be a parent. I was quite confident I would be good at it. I was a woman and I could do it, and I would do it. There was no question.'*

When we become parents somehow we cope and muddle through, looking forward to the time when we can feel really proficient in our new role. Yet, if the experience of parents when they first come to the groups is anything to go by, most of us find that we never feel proficient, that the confusions and uncertainties continue and even intensify as our children grow older. At every stage, there's a new way forward to be negotiated, a new set of choices to be made.

*'I remember when we had little children meeting a couple who had teenagers and we said, "Oh, it must be wonderful!" and they said "It isn't, a lot of the time." And we totally dismissed it. "Rubbish", we thought, "It couldn't possibly be as hard as it is now." But it is. Yes, all the excruciating physical tiredness goes, but it gets incredibly demanding on an emotional level. We're still feeling our way as much as we ever were.'*

As our children get older and start to fight free of our values – often while continuing to expect that we support and succour them — a whole new dimension of parenthood opens up. We can feel unnerved by our teenager's behaviour in ways we've not experienced with our younger children. We feel upset by their indifference and antagonism, their rejection of our values and way of life. Clashes of wills and values may be part of life with every adolescent but they can leave us very unsure about where we stand, how much influence or 'say' we can expect, or hope, for.

*'Although Bobby and I have a lot in common, he is picking up a lot of values and ideas which I don't approve of. For example, he's very impressed by money and what money can buy. At the age of twelve he is beginning to say things that make me cringe. I know it's very important not to deny his values, but occasionally there's a tremendous temptation to think, "I wish I could change it", like almost remould him somehow and make him less materialistic, but I know I don't have the right to do that.'*

'I remember before having children I'd go to the supermarket and see children at the check-out creating havoc because they wanted sweets and I'd think "Right, when I'm a parent, that won't happen to me." It was going to be the perfect relationship. And I stood in the supermarket amid seas of sweets with my son many years later going through exactly the same scene and I thought, "It can't be happening to me, I've always been so careful." '

At every stage, it can be difficult to see the way ahead. Parenthood is the most important job we ever take on, and we get no training at all, nothing to prepare us for the squabbling and the tears, the emotionally draining full-time responsibility of helping another human being to grow. Suddenly, our calm peaceful life is overturned — our beliefs are challenged, our daily routines disrupted, the amount of spare time and spare cash drastically cut back. There are days when we can feel so dominated by their strong, determined personalities we feel totally ineffectual and hopeless. And there we are acting like we always vowed we wouldn't — yelling and pleading, shouting, threatening and smacking, even *bribing* our children to be good.

'There were times before I had my own children when I was already advising other people how to bring up theirs', said pediatrician and father of two, Bruce Mann, 'I thought it was all really quite straightforward. These people who came to see me were in a mess. They weren't normal parents, like we would be. And then we had children. And we were in a mess as well.'

For all the smiles and hugs and kisses that can make up instantly for days of awfulness, parenthood can sometimes seem a thankless task. The long, hard, often uphill-seeming struggle is intensified for some mothers by the crashing loss of status as they move from independent working women to supported wives and mothers with no income or, it seems, life of their own any more. As women come to see themselves *only* as mothers, they can all too easily lose their sense of who *else* they are, beyond the full-time role they now play of homemaker, housewife and carer. It can sometimes seem as though their identity is wiped out rather than enhanced by their new role.

*'I wanted somebody to listen to what I was feeling. I found that everybody was interested in the baby — how much weight he'd gained and how often he was feeding — but nobody actually asked me how I felt, and my first child did not stop crying for months. I can remember when he was about nine months old, crawling to the health clinic and asking the health visitor if I could see the doctor. "Why, is the baby sick?" "No", I replied wearily, "but I am. I just cannot carry on any more." So I went on through to the doctor and he said, "What's the matter? The baby looks fine to me." '*

How many mothers still do the same things they enjoyed before they had children? Or make decisions about food, holidays, even clothes, and day-to-day domestic issues, based on what they *personally* want rather than what will be best for the children, even if what will be 'best' for the children is totally at odds with their own preferences? Through force of habit, many of the mothers we see in the groups have become so practised at thinking and doing for their children they have forgotten how to think and do for themselves. This can bring problems when the children go off to school full time or leave the nest. Suddenly life seems bleak, empty and meaningless without them.

The situation is different for fathers and yet often also hard: their role is shaped by their job, what 'the lads' may think life should be like, or even their own parents' views on marriage and the home. 'Part of me wanted to stay home and help with the baby', said one, 'After all, Jane's life had changed, it seemed a bit hard that I should go on as if nothing had happened. But the pressure from my friends still to meet them down at the pub after work was enormous.'

With the trend towards later and later parenthood, many new parents, mothers particularly, find with a shock that they've given up the job at which they feel competent to embrace another they feel they 'should' be able to do automatically, only to find it calls on much greater resources than their nine-to-five ever did. They discover that caring for their children does not come easily or effortlessly; that their patience is far from endless and their tempers frighteningly short. The satellite of loving support that many new mothers enjoyed in the past — parents, sisters, sisters-in-law close to home and always at hand — has been eroded by the greater isolation of modern family life. In our culture, the birth of a baby is greeted with congratulations and exclamations of delight. But once the champagne corks stop popping, and the greetings cards stop falling through the letterbox, the support often evaporates.

The common position for all politicians, whatever their party, is that of being 'for the family'. Yet, as all new parents learn to their cost, when politicians affirm their belief in the family it rarely means spending money or providing practical support. In Great Britain maternity benefits have been chipped away until they are only available to a minority of mothers. Nursery and child-care facilities are grievously under-provided. The Government has gone out of its way to stifle the office crèche movement. Britain now has just about the lowest level of financial support and childcare provision in the whole of Europe.

'It was not until I had a baby of my own, and then two, that I finally realized what the best of feminists had been bashing on about', admitted Maggie Brown, writing in *The Independent* (Friday 3 April 1987). 'As a childless optimistic career woman I conditioned myself to expect problems to arise as a series of surmountable molehills. But ... nothing I had done in the past prepared me for a total, permanent change in circumstances, or the sense of dislocation.

'I suspect I conceal it successfully but in truth I am still in a state of shock at the way British society, which had nurtured me so happily, now presents such a cold and hostile face towards that most vulnerable yet touching of all units, women with small children ... It is as if the state has decreed that child-rearing is a personal luxury, a selfish vice, unconnected with the fundamental business of continuing the species...'

With society's utter indifference ranged against them, parents and children can soon become invisible to all but each other. Instead of feeling joy, satisfaction and a sense of pride in what they do, the job of parent in the late 1980s has been so devalued that women often find themselves apologizing for being 'only mothers.' 'I haven't had another job since I've had my children', explains one mother of four, 'But when people ask me what I do, I still have to stop myself apologizing for the fact that I haven't done anything other than rear my children.'

*I had been working for ten years and met a lot of people through my job. Now, with my two-year-old son in tow, I frequently bump into old work acquaintances. 'What are you doing these days?' they ask 'Bringing up my child' I say. 'Yes, but what are you doing?'*

'Before I had Jane, I wanted to be a perfect parent. Now I just think of it in terms that I'm trying. I'm not as bad a mother as I could be. I'm doing the best I can.'

In the cold light of reality, many parents look back on the lofty standards they set themselves with a mixture of amazement and regret. Yet the ideal of the perfect mother continues to hold terrific sway. 'I'm very foggy about this role of being a mother', confessed one women in her thirties who had held down a demanding job for several years before starting her family. 'It feels like I can only be the perfect mother if I can still be professional, be efficient, look good. There just doesn't seem to be time for all that.'

Stereotypes of good and bad parents are as old as history, but it's only in recent years that the idea of Superparent has emerged in full force. 'All a parent needs to be is *more*', summed up one mother wearily, 'more understanding, more tolerant, more firm, more fun.' This is the type of parent who takes children on endless imaginative outings, dreams up inventive projects, turns discarded paper into mobiles and supervises multiplication tables in the bath.

Supermother, in this competitive brave new world, is not only super-playmate but super-teacher, seizing every chance to get her child ahead, considering everything her child does, or fails to do, as a reflection of her competence as a parent. Somehow overlooking the fact that some of the greatest geniuses in the past were slow developers (Einstein didn't say a word until he was three), the modern mother pushes her child to learn from an ever-earlier age.

*I'd taken on so much responsibility for how she turned out that every walk would be an opportunity to get her to learn something. I would point out "This is a blackberry bush" and, without even waiting for her reply, would ask her how many blackberries she could count. It was never her idea, always me pushing.'*

The threat of irreversible damage hangs heavy over modern parents, introducing a new level of anxiety unknown to previous generations whose concern for their children focussed principally on their physical health and comfort. With greater affluence and leisure, the old anxieties about feeding and clothing our children have been replaced by concerns for *their* psychological and emotional well being. These new anxieties spawn all manner of vague and terrifying fears. If we leave them to cry for a moment longer than necessary are we running the risk of permanently deforming their characters? If we mishandle the critical early stages of development are we opening the floodgates to later problems such as drug use and delinquency?

It's not just parents who are the victims of modern perfection anxiety. The pressures can rebound every bit as forcibly on their children. Mary Amersham had a revelation when she was talking heart-to-heart with Ann. 'It was lovely being able to be so honest', she reflected, 'and let her know all those things I find difficult about being a mother. And, also, it enabled her to say, "Well you've always wanted me to be so perfect", and we talked about this a lot.

I said, "Yes, I think for your sake I wanted to be the world's most perfect mother! And because of that you had to be a perfect child to prove to the world that I was a perfect mother." '

'There's an assumption that because *we* were brought up, we know how to drag the next generation up. People think it must be easy because, you know, you're a woman and it's instinctive.'

Parenthood is different for everyone. Yet, in our experience most parents share a feeling of being adrift in a world that is slow to support but quick to condemn. Too often, the advice and the books that are available reinforce all the ideals without giving effective ways of change. All parents soon get used to being confronted with a barrage of conflicting advice — from books, magazines, radio phone-ins, television, doctors, health visitors, teachers, in-laws, family and friends — and to being questioned as to the 'stage' their children have reached. They also get quite accustomed to being reproached when their infants 'fail' to achieve good weight gains and sleeping routines, and their children high enough marks at school. No matter how old the child, parenthood can be the most difficult and most demoralizing job going. Virginia Satir, a well-known family therapist, has summed it up beautifully.

'Parents teach in the toughest school in the world. You are expected to be experts on all subjects pertaining to life and living ... There are few schools to train you for your job, and there is no general agreement on the curriculum. You have to make it up yourself. Your school has no holidays, no vacations, no unions, no automatic promotions or pay rises. You are on duty or at least on call 24 hours a day, 365 days a year, for at least 18 years for each child you have ... I regard this as the hardest, most complicated, anxiety-ridden, sweat and blood producing job in the world... (*Peoplemaking*, Science and Behaviour Books Inc, USA, 1972.)

Maggie is a teacher. She finds it easy to be all the things she wants to be for her own children when she's at school — patient, encouraging, full of empathy. 'It's just part of my role as a nursery teacher to encourage the children and make them feel that their contributions are worthwhile. But as soon as I open the front door to my house, I'm confronted by a hundred thousand different things, or that's what it feels like, and my children are just a part of these hundred thousand. They never seem to have priority like the kids do at school. I just get very caught up with the supper preparations or the fact that the table still has the breakfast things on and nobody's bothered to clear it.'

Most of us, like Maggie, learn to be parents as we go along, muddling through, learning from our mistakes. We get little or no advance practice and may go into parenthood never having played with a small child or really handled a baby.

*'It was always considered that I would never have children because I was a career person, so babies weren't even handed to me when I was growing up, because I was the bright one and I wasn't you know, going to bother with that sort of thing.'*

This lack of experience is carried through as our children grow, assert their independence and start to behave in ways that mystify or appal us. What should we do? How should we deal with them? Every day, many times a day, lots of parents have to face the fact that they do not really have a clue *what* to do.

There is no clear way forward. In place of the clear-cut rules and systems of the past, there is now just a mass of conflicting ideas and philosophies: should infants be picked up the minute they wail or left to 'cry it out'? Should they be fed on demand or do they need a routine? Will a short sharp smack resolve a problem or merely intensify it? As much as the old advice seems inappropriate, so the new appears confusing and often contradictory.

Maggie, for example, who had 'rather a Victorian unbringing', was confused to find that the rules had all changed since she was a child. 'When I started bringing my own children up and meeting other mothers, I was astounded at what they let their children do. I thought, "Oh, my goodness, I'm going to have to change all my ideas." ' The old ideas just didn't translate to the reality of modern-day living. She, like other parents, felt stuck for what to replace them with.

In the absence of both guidance and current example we only have our own childhood experience to fall back on. It is the one we know best, after all. Indeed, we learn most from what was done to us. If it was happy, we may 'decide' if unconsciously to do the same.

*'I came from a really happy home and I just felt that the right*

*way to bring up children was the way that my parents had brought me up with a few modern influences thrown in.'*

If we don't decide to do more or less the same as our own parents, we tend to swing right away and resolve to go for the complete opposite.

*'Before we got married even, and certainly when Toni was pregnant, it was uppermost in our minds. We would be everything our own parents weren't. We just felt we knew we would do it right because we wouldn't do what our parents did!'*

*'I didn't know what I wanted but I knew I didn't want to do it the way they'd done it, so I was making it up all the time and not doing a wonderful job of it.'*

Even the conscious decision to avoid the things we didn't like that our parents did is no guarantee that we will be able to do it differently. The old patterns often die hard; in the absence of any clear alternative, it can take great presence of mind to stop repeating what our parents said, and did, to us.

*'I don't want to bring up my daughter the way my Mum brought me up. That's for one thing. But even sometimes when I'm talking to Ella, I can see my Mum in me. I don't like it and I try and change it to a different angle.'*

The belief amongst many people that being a mother or father is instinctive – or comes naturally – is easily shattered when we realize how important our parents were in teaching us how to behave towards our children. Certainly 50 years ago, and perhaps even 30 years ago, it was usually quite adequate for parents to repeat the pattern and bring up their children as they had been brought up, without thinking much about it.

Today, the job is not as straightforward. In the past few decades we have witnessed the failure of extremes of indulgence as well as total severity. The failure of the old disciplinarian ways may be plain to see, but it has become clear that the 'child-centered' liberalism of the fifties and sixties hasn't provided many answers either. Dr Benjamin Spock championed the radical new thinking that children should be brought up never to be limited or frustrated. But, tellingly, he gradually revised his ideas through subsequent editions of his bestselling *Baby and Child Care* (Bodley Head, 1979) as it became clear that allowing the child's will unlimited sway could be just as undesirable as ruling with a rod of iron. The only difference was that instead of the parent tyrannizing the child, the child was tyrannizing the parent.

The challenge of taking the middle road, where children are guided with loving firmness to develop their own sense of responsibility, where they are not so much disciplined but encouraged to become self-disciplined, is a hard one. It's much easier to stick to one of the two extremes because our route is then set. Negotiating the middle way makes continual demands on our personal judgement, so much so that we often feel at a loss.

Increasingly we find others making our minds up for us. Politicians call for a return to discipline, the three R's and learning by rote and teachers argue that they should be responsible for the moral and sex education and socializing of our children. Consequently, more and more parents feel left out in the cold, confused and concerned for the most useful ways to live with their children and help them develop successfully into happy, responsible adults.

---

## Feeling good about yourself

In today's over-critical climate it's easy to feel demoralized about your abilities as a parent. Opportunities for feeling good about what you do are probably all too rare. Think now of at least one thing that makes you feel good about yourself as a parent — something you do or have done for your child that felt or feels special. Examples might be arranging a birthday party, reading or playing games, giving hugs.

---

## 'I think if I told my ex-husband I was involved with something like this, support groups for parents, he'd have me committed!'

For most people, the idea of getting some support both appeals and puts off. On the one hand, we feel we need all the help we can get, and, on the other, we feel we should be perfectly capable of doing it on our own. We shouldn't *need* help. Parenthood is perfectly natural, after all. People have managed to raise children without the aid of books and courses ever since the human race began.

*'I can remember being a bit surprised that a friend of mine was looking at psychology books about how children learn things in stages, and thinking, "Books!" It didn't seem quite right somehow. I suppose I felt that being a parent was something that you just did and, if you didn't just do it, there was something wrong that would need more than a book to put right.'*

'If I went to a parents' group it would show me up as an inadequate mother', said one of the women we interviewed for our research when planning our parent support groups. 'I would think I was a failure if I needed help and support. I should be able to manage on my own.'

She roundly rejected the whole idea of joining a support group for parents; others overcome their initial reservations. 'I was very anti the idea to begin with', remembers Judy Francis, a single parent with two young children. 'I always thought mothering was natural. All you needed to do was follow your instincts and do the best you could. That was the ethos I was brought up on, "Do the best you can. You can't do more." But now I think with knowledge you can do more.'

At our parent support groups, we believe that sharing experiences can give new insights and that questioning how we are with our children can help to improve the quality of family life. After all, it is through questioning that people's lives evolve into something better than they were. Workers' questioning has led to better treatment and conditions; women questioning is leading slowly to a change in how they are regarded in the world; parents and children questioning together could lead to some of the most fundamental changes our society has seen.

Most parents join our parent support groups because they are looking for a general way forward rather than help with a specific problem.

*'I didn't think I had any really deep problems with my children, though I accepted there were areas with room for improvement. I have always had a zest for learning and for new ideas and I thought that whatever happened I would come out at the end a wiser and maybe even a better parent.'*

Others, prompted by specific difficulties and problems, are quite consciously looking for new ways in place of the old.

*'We were doing things which we were not happy about doing. They didn't feel right, and they certainly weren't getting the results we wanted, but we didn't*

*know of any other way. We found ourselves constantly in no-win situations in which we were having to do things which didn't feel right for lack of an alternative. Through our parent support group we learned another way.'*

People coming to the groups soon discover that everyone is struggling with some aspect of family life, an illustration of the old Chinese proverb, 'Nobody's family can hang out the sign "Nothing the matter here." ' They also find that support and education for parents does not mean having instant answers provided for them, but finding answers for themselves. In view of the huge variety in people's circumstances and values, anything else would, we believe, be impossible and probably foolish. There are many different ways of dealing with problems that parents come up against.

*'For me there is a huge difference between finding an expert who will give me endless well-meaning advice about what I should do, and spending time with a group of parents, some like me, some very different, learning other ways to respond to my children and handle the family upsets, without anyone breathing down my neck or telling me dogmatically what's right or wrong.'*

## 'It's a really big job helping and guiding the children along. Sometimes I feel it's overwhelming. You can never do it adequately.'

Even as we consider how to provide support for parents, it is worth bearing in mind that children need new aspects of support from their parents compared to the young of previous generations. Life, for them, is very different from the secure, safe place we knew when we were young; much more threatening, full of rapidly changing fads and social expectations, great competition for approval, position, even educational places and ultimately jobs.

*'I was struggling hard to persuade my son of the need to do well in his 'A' levels so he would win a university place and be assured of a good job. Nothing seemed more important to me, yet I was getting nowhere. I brought the problem up in my parent support group and with the coordinator's help I began to see things from his point of view. A degree was no longer any kind of guarantee of a job. To him, the whole future looked bleak. He*

*felt as if he had no prospects, was destined for a life on the dole, worthless in the eyes of everybody. The more pressure I put on him, the more pessimistic he felt. I was, in effect, making it impossible for him to start broadening his horizons and find an optimistic way ahead, just by insisting that what had been right for me twenty-five years ago must be right for him now.'*

Even at the most basic practical level, the old securities are frequently not there any more.

*'My family have lived in the same house since 1947 whereas Mary has lived in three different houses in her first eight years. There is much more movement. It feels like a completely different emotional world...'*

*'When I was a child, I went through primary and most of secondary school with the same close friends. They became chums for life, people whom I knew I could really rely on, real friends! My children now don't have any real friends. They have changed schools twice in five years and each time we have lived a car journey from the school, so spending time with school chums is difficult outside school hours. Their circle of friends is non-existent com-*

*pared to mine as a youngster.'*

There's an entirely new youth culture most parents know little about, unless they make the effort to find out. Now that the stories and fairy-tales that were passed down from generation to generation have more or less disappeared, parents can find themselves increasingly out of touch with their children. This is intensified by the

fact that, as children have become consumers with spending power of their own, the manufacturers of toys and games are increasingly bypassing the parents and addressing children directly — advertising in comics and children's television times.

*'At Christmas and birthdays, John works out, well in advance, exactly what his dues are. He'll say, "You bought me that last year, this year I'd like this and it's ten pounds and twenty two p more, will that matter?" That to me can spoil Christmas. He's nine. I've some idea in my head that a child shouldn't be materialistic, although of course when I go shopping I am constantly counting what I can have, and what I can't.'*

Children cannot help but be acutely aware of what everyone else has and they haven't. 'It's incredibly bombarding' summed up one mother. 'Sandra comes home each day with a list of different things she's seen which she wants us to buy for her, all from different programmes on TV. It's like an avalanche, you can't stop it.' She is anxious, like so many parents, that the influence of home is being overridden by the influence of school and increasingly television — aspects over which any parent can only have limited control.

---

## How well do you know your child?

Are you aware of what is going on in your children's world, what their influences are and what's important to them? Do you know what their favourite stories, comics, music, TVs and videos are? Do you have any idea of the plots or who the heroes and villains are? Do you know which authority figures they like and why? Who their friends are and what they like about them?

---

This generation of children is at once over-protected and frighteningly over-exposed to all kinds of new influences. It's a strange mixture of being kept a child, with no real part to play in the adult world, and being a pseudo grown-up.

*'On one hand Jilly already wants to wear high heels and make-up and she's only eight. And on the other hand, I dare not let her out on her own. When I was young I'd go out and if I wasn't seen for several hours it didn't matter. Now Jilly has to let me know exactly where she's going to be and if for some reason she's in*

*the park on her own, I start to worry, thinking "Where is she?" '*

Now that they are exposed to so much so young, children, more than ever, need their own resources to withstand the presssure from children their own age or older, resisting the invitation to bunk school, start smoking or behave in anti-social ways. Pressure from their own age group may determine whether they stay on at school or take a relatively menial job as the first step on the employment ladder, start experimenting with drugs or alcohol, or embark on sexual relationships and run the risks of unwanted pregnancy or even developing diseases, such as AIDS.

Secure teenagers will be able to resist the group pressure that feels wrong to them but the less secure may allow themselves to be pushed into doing things they know are wrong in order to gain approval or simply remain accepted. Providing our children with support means helping them develop enough inner strength to speak up for themselves rather than going along with the crowd.

They need belief in themselves not to be swayed by the arguments of older or more influential children.

As the world gets more dangerous and threatening, it's more important than ever that children do have a strong solid base inside themselves; that they know it's OK to say 'No' if a situation makes them feel threatened or uncomfortable; that they can act in an independent way rather than just going along with whatever is suggested. This way they develop not just a healthy regard for themselves but a possibly life-saving instinct for self-preservation. Campaigns like the American anti-drug initiative, 'Just Say NO', underestimate how very difficult some individuals find it not to comply with whatever is suggested to them — whether it's taking drugs, sleeping with an insistent boyfriend or going off with a stranger. 'I was brought up with "Don't you dare say "No' " and I have trouble with saying it even now', said one woman, who was herself abducted as a young girl. Now she realizes how vitally important it is her daughter gets different messages and learns a different way.

'I feel it is important to involve myself with Miles. My father never had the time or the inclination to. As far as I could make out, he spent twenty-four hours a day earning a living.'

It's not just the world outside the home that's different – family life is changing too. The family may be a great sanctuary from the often harsh reality of life, but it is also a great sanctuary for myths — particularly the seductive vision of the past, when father and mother knew their places, grandma and grandpa were just down the road and AIDS, anorexia and drug addiction were unheard of.

There is no such thing as a typical family any more, with father out at work and mum at home looking after the children. Instead there are lots of families, including many more single-parent families: the number has doubled in the last 20 years and is still rising.

Even in the most nuclear-type of family, the roles of mother, father, parent, wife, husband, worker and nurturer are all slowly being reinterpreted. More men push prams, change nappies, help with the housework, attend PTA meetings and talk to teachers. More women go out to work and help with the household expenses.

As this happens more and more, so the image of man as father as provider and nominal head of the family has relaxed. At home, now, men routinely carry out tasks that their fathers would not have dreamt of undertaking.

'My feeling about being a dad was somebody who worked too hard and was exhausted all the time', said one father, whose own father had only ever featured in family life as an absent threat: 'Just wait till your father gets home!!' He welcomes the chance to take a more active part in the life of his family.

As men and women look for companionship and equality and seek more fulfilling relationships between themselves, so they are also changing their ideas about the sort of relationship they want with their children; searching for ways of being authoritative without being authoritarian and guiding them as they grow in a manner that respects the autonomy and independence of their offspring.

*'When the children were little they respected us just because we were their parents. Now I know that the more we try to hold on to being "Parents", demanding their respect from a position of strength, the more likely they are to rebel against it. We have to earn their respect just as they do ours.'*

These changes in attitude are also encouraged, if not demanded, by the children themselves. Children see their mothers, or other children's mothers, standing up for their rights in the home and at work. They witness their teachers striking for more pay and questioning their rights in the school as workplace. It is hardly surprising that children have themselves begun to question their position both in the family and at school. Objecting to how they are treated by parents and teachers is no longer the province of teenagers. Younger and younger children are questioning parental decisions and family rules, demanding in their most awkward and persuasive ways to have their views, needs and rights taken into account. Far from being seen and not heard, many of the younger generation are now standing up to be counted in the unlikeliest of places.

*'I hate the way adults think they are better than children! They don't listen to our opinions, ask us what we want or let us have our say, just ignore us as if we don't count.' (A twelve year old.)*

Children themselves are being revealed as a new class whose legal rights and real emotional, physical and psychological needs are emerging in greater detail than ever before. In many ways, they are the last unacknowledged oppressed minority. There is no commission for age equality or equal opportunities for young people, no minister for childhood or even junior under-secretary to consider what the children of the late twentieth century might need in our rapidly changing world. At home and at school, there are frighteningly few people willing and available to listen to what they feel or want.

Fortunately, there are signs that this situation is (slowly) changing, that parents and adults generally are becoming much more aware of the injustices and inequalities many children suffer.

Our own research, conducted independently after the launch of our parent support organization in June 1986, clearly showed that many modern parents place a high value on enjoying more equal relationships with their children. They recognize that they are very different from their children and yet, for all that, they believe that their children are equally important. They want their children to feel that their feelings and opinions count and that, regardless of how young they are, they will be treated with equal consideration rather than brushed aside and dismissed.

'It's not a very comfortable thing to have power over somebody less strong than you', said one father, grateful now to have experienced new ways of negotiating differences with his children other than 'those awful kind of brittle battles' where he would end up pulling rank.

*'My children are much freer to say what they think to us than I*

*was. We lived in an atmosphere where children were to be seen and not heard. I was very frightened of my Father and could never be close to my Mother. I couldn't confide in her and can't even now. I knew that I didn't want my children to feel the way I felt. I want them to have a nice, relaxed relationship with me where they can come and talk to me about anything. I want them to feel that they are respected, that their feelings and opinions count.'*

This idea of equality is not to be confused with sameness. For all their rapid developments these days, children are still children. They do not have the experience, knowledge or physical maturity to take the same degree of responsibility for their own lives as adults are required to take. Nevertheless, they do have needs, views and feelings which can be taken into account as equally worthy of respect and consideration.

*'We were about to move house when I joined the group. One day it struck me that Ann sees our house as being her house too, so I'm now taking her to see houses that I'm thinking of living in. Before, I wouldn't have thought of consulting her in a serious sense. I might have taken her along if she was interested, but I wouldn't have considered her*

*views. I might have said, "As from next Wednesday you're living in such and such a place . . ." or "Tomorrow the removal van is coming." '*

*'I can remember my parents saying, "I've been around more years than you, I know better than you", and it used to fill me with such bitterness and resentment. I remember feeling that what we felt and wanted counted for nothing. My Mother said she stopped reading to us because we weren't interested. But that wasn't true. We weren't interested in what she chose to read to us – we were never consulted about what we wanted to hear. So to this day she maintains we weren't interested in reading or stories. We were "no good" with books.'*

The interviews and group discussions carried out during the course of our research indicated that the aspirations of modern parents have shifted away from achievement-oriented goals towards more personal qualities, such as happiness, contentment, fulfilment, stability, independence, self-assurance and confidence.

Interestingly, in times of such high unemployment, not one parent mentioned a specific career he or she cherished for their child. Although most expressed the hope that their children would have a

## How do your children see you?

What is it like to be a child? Somewhere inside we all know because we have been one. Take a few moments to think, and ask yourself how you would have liked your parents to have been with you? Did they respect your views and opinions, take what you thought and felt seriously? Did they give you the warm, close, loving kind of attention you needed?

Now consider what is it like to be your son or your daughter? What is it like for them to have you as a parent?

job and a reasonable standard of living, they did not want this at the expense of all the rest. 'I'd like to give them the skills to survive', said one mother, 'but, on the other hand, I don't want to encourage a world where children are beating each other over the head to get ahead.'

Above all, these parents expressed the wish that their children should have an idea of their own value, that they should feel confident and competent, and have high self-esteem; not in the sense of being cocky or insensitive to the plight and problems of others but just knowing they mattered as human beings. These parents wanted their children to grow up feeling valued for themselves rather than for what they might or might not manage to 'achieve' in the world's eyes. For their own part, they hoped to be able to give their children a sense of who they were, where they wished to go with their lives and to help them develop the necessary strengths and qualities to enable them to move in their chosen direction.

Children need to know they are loved, capable of coping with life and have something to contribute right from the time they are very small. It's now generally recognized that the way individuals feel about themselves as children largely determines how they will feel about themselves as adults — whether they will have a high or a low opinion about themselves, consider themselves worthwhile or worthless, lovable or unlovable, competent or a failure. Such considerations will influence their lives and relationships at every level, determining everything from how easily they deal with hardships and setbacks to the kinds of friends they make, the career they choose and how trusting they are of others.

The part that parents play in this process can hardly be over-estimated. Through their words, actions and, above all, their attitudes, parents communicate their trust and confidence in their child and the child picks it up. If he does not get the feeling from them that he is a worthwhile and capable individual, it will be very hard for him to acquire that confidence later on in life.

## Self-esteem
Children need to get positive messages about:

- **Being**
  Their right to be here, the fact that they are lovable and worthwhile just because they exist.

  We convey this by saying things like, 'I love you', 'I'm glad you're here', 'I enjoy being with you'. Actions and gestures also convey these feelings: hugs and kisses, spending time with them and really listening to what they have to tell us often speak louder than words.

- **Doing**
  Their ability to contribute, the fact that they are capable and can do well.

  We can get this across by expressing appreciation of their talents, saying 'You did that well!' or 'I really liked the way you did that' (and say what it is); by noting what they do right as well as (or instead of) what they get wrong, 'That's great, you remembered you left your homework behind and took on the responsibility for coming back to get it'; by pointing to their past strengths and achievements, when they are feeling low about some present disappointment or failure. 'Remember that time you organized that surprise play for Dad's birthday, you were really pleased about that!'

- **Thinking**
  Their ability to work things out for themselves, to feel confident enough to express their views and feelings in the knowledge that they will be listened to and their opinions considered.

  We can take the time to listen and take account of their ideas and points of view. 'I like the way you thought that through' 'That's interesting. What makes you think that?'

'I hear myself talking to my children in a way that I would never talk to other adults and friends. And I love my children. I mean they are much more precious to me than other adults. But I talk to them in such an offensive way sometimes. And yet if they do that to me, all hell's let loose!'

Wanting more democratic relationships inside the family is one thing. Achieving them is quite another. As we have seen, the force of our own upbringing is so strong that it leaves deeply-ingrained patterns and attitudes we may not even be aware of.

The cultural tendency to believe that parents always know best is not easily shaken off. Yet, if we are to achieve more equal relationships with our children, we have to face up to the fact that we, as parents, are not the authority on everything. Not only do we not have all the answers but our children may have answers that we don't. Even very young children.

Michael Johnson is just over a year old. 'I trust him to know what he wants', said his mother who used to have the most fearful battles over meals with his older sister, Susan. 'I still find it difficult to believe sometimes that he knows what's best for him, but every time he shows me I get a little more trusting. I've noticed these huge differences in his appetite, for example. One day he will eat huge amounts of food; the next he doesn't want any. He shakes his head or pushes the bowl away or throws his bottle out over the side of his cot. And that's the end of it. It's no big deal. If he's hungry, well, he's going to let me know. I found a couple of times when he didn't want any supper at all, I would think "Does he know what he's doing, how can he go for twelve hours without food?" But he knew. He didn't wake up, he slept right through.

'With Susan, I thought I was being very democratic, or at least I was being as democratic as I knew how. I'd ask her what she wanted, and how much, and then when she wouldn't eat it we'd spend an hour or more sitting there furious with each other — me determined not to give way for fear of where it would all lead.'

Parents with attitudes as open as this are very rare. Most adults cannot bring themselves to believe that their children can know what they need. Every day on the street, on the TV, in the playground, even in our own houses, we hear ourselves or others dismissing or brushing aside what children say, contradicting what they tell us, not accepting the way they feel.

- 'Of course you don't hate the new baby . . .'
- 'You don't want another ice-cream, you've only just finished that one . . .'
- 'Don't be silly. There isn't a monster in the bedroom. Now snuggle down and go to sleep . . .'

We may 'put our children right' when they tell us certain things, sincerely believing that it will minimize their distress and make everything all right.

- 'There's nothing to be upset about . . .'
- 'Of course you like your teacher . . .'

The classic way of denying children's feelings of hurt, anger or upset — as every parent uncomfortably recognizes — is to say that they are 'tired'. But our own experience should tell us that children bitterly resent being *told* that they feel one way when they feel quite the opposite and have already taken the trouble to tell us as much: 'I am *not* tired!'

Allowing children to have feelings that we'd prefer they didn't have is all part of the new language of acceptance. Acknowledging painful and difficult feelings, however alarming or trivial they seem to us, is to accept our children's own independence, the fact that they are quite separate from us, rather than trying to direct their experience or to speak 'for' them:

- 'How old are you now?'
  'He's six'

In the groups, parents soon find it's hard to unlearn attitudes they've been living with for a lifetime and to move towards more equal relationships, especially when they've been used to laying down the law all the time. Through the long, hard struggle towards change — becoming more the sort of parent we would like to be more of the time — our children can, surprisingly, prove our greatest allies. Even when treated unfairly, they display a forgivingness and ungrudgingness almost absent in our adult world.

*'If I treated my friends the way I do my children, I would have probably lost them for life. But my children come back. Next morning, a few hours later, they've forgotten about all the horrible things I've done. They still love me. That used to be quite a surprise.'*

The marvellous part of being a

parent is that the relationship can always be improved. We all know the bad patches, when we scream and shout and behave exactly like the parents we vowed we'd never be and we all know too that even at those times where we feel as if everything is irredeemably spoilt, we always get another chance. Our children forgive us. With goodwill, openness and honesty, the willingness to experiment and try new ways, better times are just around the corner.

Yet, even as we aim for things to be better than they already are, take a moment to recall the many joyful moments that you have shared with your children. It is all too easy sometimes to get stuck in concern over the bad patches and to ignore the pleasant ones!

'Joseph was a page at a wedding in the summer and we'd been *trying hard to explain to him what a page was, and he'd got the idea, and all was well, until he was sitting on my knee as usual at bedtime, listening to a story, and I said, "You turn the page", and he said, "I am the page!"'*

*'My son had been using me as a punch bag and I suggested reading a book as a break for me! Halfway through the book about fathers and their children I asked him, "What do you think dads are for?" His reply was "For loving and taking care of."'*

*'My daughter had not long started school. The whole family was sitting around at home one day when she announced, "You know when I'm grown up I'm going to live in the house next door to you so that our children can play together."'*

## Summary

• Most of us embark on parenthood with no preparation, little practice nor any clear idea about the type of parents we'd like to be.

• The reality can come as a shock, leaving us feeling incompetent, ineffectual and hopeless. These feelings are reinforced by the deep-seated cultural expectation that parenthood is instinctive and comes naturally: we should just be able to do it.

• Despite all the rewards, the day-to-day grind, particularly for mothers, can seem overwhelming at times — so overwhelming that they lose sight of who else they are other than cleaner, washer, provider of meals, play leader, lavatory attendant . . .

- The general lack of support for parents, political and social, can give a feeling of being adrift in a world that is slow to support but quick to condemn.

- Unlike our parents and grandparents, we no longer have any clear guidelines to follow, just lots of different and conflicting ideas and philosophies.

- Lack of any clear idea about how to proceed, and force of habit, means we often fall back on following what our parents did, whether or not that's what we want.

- Getting help and support from a group of parents like ourselves, with a guiding coordinator, enables us to explore new options and gives us alternative ways of responding.

- Getting support ourselves enables us to support our children and give them what they need. This may be very different from what we needed as children. After all, it's a very different world out there.

- Children need confidence in themselves above all; the inner strength and self-esteem to resist pressures from other children, and say 'no' to those suggestions that feel wrong, whether it's an invitation to try drugs or the advance of a stranger.

- As children witness their parents and others outside the family striving towards more equal relationships, they want a part in it too. Many parents also wish to treat their children more democratically, to be authoritative without being authoritarian, but are stuck for ways to do so.

- Enjoying more equal relationships with our children means questioning some of our most deeply-held attitudes and assumptions, letting them have more responsibility for their own lives, respecting their feelings and opinions.

- Children often help us, by insisting that they be heard and not allowing us to override their ideas. They are also extraordinarily forgiving of our lapses, and so help us to change into the type of parents we'd like to be more of the time.

# CHAPTER 2

# THEIR NEEDS, OUR NEEDS

'My youngest son had a teddy that always slept in bed with him. One night I went in to say "goodnight" and found teddy slung out of the bottom of the bed. So I said "Hey, just a minute, your teddy's here . . ." and he said, "Oh, it's all right, Mum, he doesn't need me any more"!'

Tiny newborn infants can do nothing for themselves. They depend on us totally for their survival. When they cry, we comfort them; when they are hungry, we feed them; when they are dirty, we change and bathe them. For the first year or so of life, these needs totally shape our lives; all our activities are either organized around what they need or their needs stage-managed in order to make other activities possible.

But with each day, and each month, children become more capable of leading their own lives and meeting their own needs — whether it's holding their own cup and spoon to feed, wriggling over to face the other way, crawling to retrieve a toy or taking on the responsibility of getting themselves to school on time.

*'Now the boys are a bit older, I'm gradually reclaiming a bit more of my own life. When they were very little, their needs came first practically all of the time.'*

An important aspect of our understanding and skill as parents concerns just how much responsibility we can usefully encourage our children to take as they slowly develop, learn to walk, talk, feed and dress themselves. As they grow, each at their own rate, children move from a state of total dependence, when we are one hundred per cent responsible for them, to a state of total (theoretical) independence, whereby they are one hundred per cent responsible for themselves. Although our children can always be seen as equal to us in terms of their *value* as human beings, their degree of independence must inevitably depend on their level of physical and emotional development — with us relinquishing control and them taking it on as we, and they, feel ready.

As our children grow, our role as a parent changes. Our early responsibility is clearly that of provider, protector and nurturer — caretaker of all needs, sorter out of all crises. But as our children get a little older, they have call on us in other ways — to guide and to teach, to entertain and illuminate, to be close to and confide in.

At each stage, the old roles need gradually to be rethought and sometimes relinquished as new ones are taken on. Parenthood demands that we continually and flexibly adapt our responses according to the developing abilities of our growing child. Sometimes, however, we remain stuck in one role well after the time has come to change, underestimating our children's capacity and desire for responsibility and so continuing to do more for them than is necessary or even desirable. We know, or think we know, our children so well that we stop updating our information about them — forgetting that they are constantly developing and changing. When our children are very small, their triumphs are unmistakable. But when they get older, the process of change is easier to miss because it tends to take place on a more subtle emotional level.

'I have to keep on reminding myself that people, especially teenage people, are capable of taking decisions and looking after themselves', said Mary Amersham, who had been watching her thirteen-year-old daughter, Ann, doing handstands on the grass. 'When Ann fell over, my immediate reaction was to rush to her. My baby was hurt. But she said quite firmly, "I am *not* your baby. You do not have to come and make my foot better. When I'm at school doing gym and I hurt myself, I just have to get on with it." '

Many parents would get hopelessly stuck in time warps, constantly over protecting and rushing to the rescue, were it not for the fact that their children assert their own separateness and independence so relentlessly that they *have* to take notice. From the time they are tiny, children make it blindingly clear that they have their own lives to lead, with wills and ideas of their own, which they will often try to assert against us. When we step in and take over, they may not thank us for our 'help'. Indeed, they often resent it strongly.

One couple, Maria and Bill, came

to the group after a weekend spent taking their three-year-old on an outing to the train museum. After a very happy time climbing in and out of trains and having rides, it was time to go home. They went out via the postcard stall. 'And there were all these postcards of trains', explained Bill. 'So we stopped and I picked out a few for him. But he got more and more uptight and started screaming. I was saying "For God's sake shut up. OK, THAT'S IT!! We'll go home", when Maria came up and asked him what was wrong. It turned out that all he wanted was to pick the postcard out himself. She gave him a few pence and he picked out the tattiest one there and calmed down immediately. In fact he was running around with delight he was so pleased, and what had been a bad situation suddenly turned out to be a good one.'

Older children can be just as adamant that they do not want us acting 'on their behalf'.

*'I was concerned about how Anita was getting on with the other pupils in her new school and had already been in to talk to her teacher. But I was still getting a feeling that things were not quite right. I was about to march off to school again when I thought I'd try talking to her about it first. To my utter astonishment, Anita's main worry was that I would interfere with what was going on in school for her. She definitely did not want me talking to her teacher without her permission.'*

Most parents in the groups say they can remember times when they were embarrassed or upset by something their own parents did, or said, usually in the most well-meaning attempt to help. It's worth bearing in mind that our over-involvement as parents can sometimes compound the difficulties our children are going through or may even be the cause of them.

## 'Nine-tenths of the growing away I celebrate, but there is the one tenth that fills me with a kind of regret.'

As we are gradually released from the old chores — the full-time job of caretaker and comfort giver — the enormous sense of satisfaction we feel at our children's achievements may be coupled with a pang of loss as every new step takes them a little further away from us and other people become important in their lives and other influences paramount.

*'I preferred it when she was three and if I wanted her with me, all I had to do was pick her up. In a way I did what I wanted, and it was easier than living with this growing-up person who more and more does as she wants to do.'*

There are times when all parents feel unsure and out-of-step, unable to give their children what they now feel they need. Fraser Harrison has put it well in his autobiographical writings. 'When the children were babies, their needs more or less determined our way of life and defined our identity, but as they became schoolchildren I stumbled into a void. I still needed them to give shape and meaning to my life, but now they needed me in ways I could not satisfy. I had surprised myself, and probably everyone else, by being a proficient and patient motherfather, but when it came to being a parent of children who had outgrown nappies and required a more sophisticated level of help and education, I felt I was failing them. The more they asked of me — and they asked for nothing out of the ordinary — the more conscious I became of my inadequacy.' (*A Winter's Tale*, Collins, 1987.)

As our children grow, it is hard to know how much freedom to give them — and when. When are they old enough to go to the local shop alone? When will it be alright for them to stay up late, or overnight, at a friend's house? As each situation arises, a new decision has to be made.

It is not as clear as it used to be when children become adults. In one sense, they grow up frighteningly fast. In another, they are kept 'children' for longer than was usual in the past, or indeed is usual now in other cultures where even very young children contribute to the general day-to-day existence in tangible and important ways — carrying water, looking after livestock, fetching wood, caring for their younger brothers and sisters.

In many societies, important rituals clearly mark the passage of child to man or woman. In the Jewish tradition, for example, the coming of age is celebrated with ceremonial introductions into the community of adults. In Britain, meanwhile, kids just get given the key to the door at eighteen. There are, of course, several legal definitions about what children are, or are not, considered able to do when.

# Thresholds of responsibility

At birth, you can open a bank account; at forty-eight hours you can sue someone for being born disabled or deformed; at five years you can enter a cinema and drink intoxicating liquor with a meal in a restaurant but you cannot buy it or be served it; at twelve you can buy a pet; at thirteen you can do light work during holiday time or weekends provided that it's not before 7 am or after 7 pm; at fourteen, you can pawn your possessions; at sixteen you can marry, fly solo in a glider, buy fireworks and horror comics, refuse or consent to medical treatment and join a trade union; at seventeen you can trade in the streets; at eighteen you can change your name, vote and make a will, carry a donor card and give your organs away, serve on a jury, can be tattooed or hanged for treason; at twenty-one you can adopt a child . . .

In family life these thresholds of responsibility are not nearly so clear cut. If we look at some of the day-to-day tasks that we are doing 'for' our children, we probably find several they might start doing for themselves at levels fitting their abilities.

How about:

- Choosing and preparing the food that they want
- Choosing and taking care of their clothes
- Operating household equipment — cookers, fires, telephones, videos and hi-fi, washers and driers.
- Having arguments with siblings, friends, the other parent
- Looking after their toys and possessions
- Tidying, cleaning and decorating their areas of the house
- Touching and exploring their bodies
- Choosing friends, interests, reading material, music and television programmes
- Going out alone
- Travelling alone on buses, trains and planes
- Shopping — for them and for you
- Spending money — yours and/or theirs

When one of the parents in the groups set her mind on all the things she was doing for her child that he might be doing for himself, she gained so many new insights she made a new resolution.

'I realized that I didn't have to look for my little boy's lost toys any longer. They were his, he lost them, he could find them. What a revelation! I had been doing it for months and not really wanting to and resenting it greatly without realizing it. I told him I didn't like having to do it and that I wasn't going to any longer. From now on he was in charge of his own toys.

'He cried, he got angry, he told me that I would forget about it, and carry on doing it (which was a fatal thing to say!) and he stamped around and did what he called "nasty things" to me. I listened to him and helped him cope with his upset feelings whilst still sticking to my decision. AND HE FOUND HIS OWN THINGS. And I found at least two hours a day more for myself. And I no longer resent him and his lost toys. And he is beginning not to lose things. Now what else am I doing for him, that I don't want or don't need to?'

Ros Brown also decided it was time her daughter, Susan, had more responsibility for deciding when she was going to go to sleep. 'I was bored of popping my head round the door to check the light was out. So we agreed that as long as she got ready for bed by a certain time and

was in her bedroom, she could turn her light out when she wanted. But, you know, when I put the idea forward she didn't trust me! I said "You can turn your light out." She said suspiciously, "What do you mean?" So I repeated it and she said "Does that mean you're going to come along and check?" And I said "No". So now she does it herself and you know, I've noticed that her light seems to go off pretty close to when it always used to anyway!'

## 'She's the most wonderful mother, what she doesn't do for her children!'

Encouraging children to do more for themselves seems wrong to some parents. They feel that it's their job to provide tirelessly for their children — to solve their problems, answer their questions, help with their homework. After all, that's what parents are there for. They can put themselves under an impossible pressure, making sure their children are happy all the time.

*'Jane would come out with "It's not fair, Sarah's going to a party." And I'd do whatever I could to make it all right for her, to think of some special treat she could have in its place. I felt it was down to me to deal with her disappointment. The result was we soon got into an impossible situation where she expected everything to be made equal.'*

The 'good' self-sacrificing all-giving mother that gives other parents such complexes is not necessarily acting in her child's best interests. By doing everything for her child, she keeps him helpless, postponing the time when he'll finally have to learn how to do things for himself. The 'good enough' mother knows that she helps most by not helping, by making herself dispensable.

When we allow a child to climb up onto fences and gates, trusting his sense of balance and knowledge of his own limits, we communicate a confidence in his own abilities far more powerful than we could have done by insisting he hold our hand; when we listen to his upsets without telling him what to do we let him know we think him capable of sorting them out himself. Obviously we need to use our judgement to decide what our children are capable of when, and there are great risks involved in over-protecting them; doing everything for them

## 'Good' v 'good enough'

- The 'good' parent makes decisions for her child
- The 'good enough' parent encourages her child to take his own decisions, starting with small things like what to wear. This shows respect for the child's decision-making abilities and his right to an independent point of view

- The 'good' parent does everything for her child
- The 'good enough' parent lets her child do things for himself that he is capable of doing and shows enthusiasm for, such as cleaning the bath, even though he may not do the perfect job she would have done

- The 'good' parent protects her child from making mistakes
- The 'good enough' parent allows her child to learn from the consequences of his own actions and inactions. If he is always forgetting to take his packed lunch to school, she doesn't run after him but lets him learn from the experience so helping him to remember next time

for the first sixteen to eighteen years of their lives, saving them from the unpleasant yet useful mistakes that they could be learning from. How many to day's school leavers are adequately equipped to live in the real world?

*'As a child, I tagged along behind my parents as they chose my clothes, my books, my school, even my friends. I played no part in decisions about what the family did, was given no say in where we went on holiday, what we ate, how we spent the family money. Then at eighteen I left home, got a job and was totally unprepared to fend for myself, take sensible decisions, look after my income and new flat. Now, I realize that I can, and must, involve my children in most of the things that happen in our home. They are active partners in this family with strong views, likes, hates and contributions to make.'*

Within reasonable limits, the more free rein we give our children, the more able they will be to start fending for themselves in the world. Giving children responsibility for looking after themselves, and letting them know that we believe them capable of it, gives them confidence in their own abilities and helps them gain valuable practice for later life.

'Sometimes I say, "Well I would love to be able to let you sit there and count all the spiders, but we really have to go now so will you just hurry up." '

Most of us are in so much of a rush that it seems quicker and easier to continue to do everything ourselves rather than let our children explore and discover in their own time. It's easier, and certainly faster, to wake them in the mornings and get them dressed, do up their buttons, zip up their coats, remind them to take their homework and ship them off to school.

Ultimately, of course, fostering an independent spirit saves time. As our children take on the tasks we still might be doing for them, such as washing their hair or finding their toys, they will get more practised and more competent and we will no longer be required to chivvy them along. This releases us from the bind of having to live their lives as well as ours, giving us more time for ourselves.

Children need to proceed at their own pace in order to learn. In the Slade household, Pat's time is taken up first thing in the mornings giving physiotherapy to her older daughter who has cystic fibrosis. This means that the younger one,

Sarah, has about twenty minutes when she is awake and doing nothing. 'One day, I was doing Jane's physio, when Sarah came in dressed. I couldn't believe it. Here was this child not yet two, fully dressed. There had been no fights about what she was going to wear or how she was going to put it on. She had the time to struggle with her trousers. If both legs went in one leg, it wasn't me saying "Oh, come on, hurry up, I'll do it for you." She had time to learn how to dress herself. In fact she's the only one of her contemporaries who *can* dress herself.'

*'Alex was not quite three when we went on a holiday. Each time we got into the car he wanted to shut the door behind him. This meant him having to pull the door within six inches of shut while standing in the road, then climbing in and pulling it the rest of the way. Often I would have to give it another push from the outside just to make sure it was fully closed. After a*

*while, I got quite impatient until a friend pointed out that we were not actually in a hurry. What was wrong with Alex taking two minutes to get into the car whilst enjoying himself and learning something new?'*

Some parents worry that handing over more responsibility to their children will mean abandoning them to muddle through entirely on their own. Fortunately, there is much we can do between the extremes of taking over and ignoring them completely. Most helpfully, perhaps, we can let them decide how they would like *us* to help *them*. When they agree to be responsible for being out of the house at ten past eight every morning, for example, we can ask how we can help them keep to that deadline. They might find it valuable if we act as time-keeper and give a ten minute warning or lend them an alarm clock set for 8.05.

*'My daughter had been given a kitten for Chrismas and now, nine months later, she was regularly forgetting to feed it. I challenged her about it and she asked for help in remembering. Between us we came up with several ideas, including thoroughly cleaning out several empty cat food tins and hanging them on the inside of her bedroom door – so they would clatter and remind her when she got in from school.'*

'My kids never cleared the table. They left everything for me because I was always doing it. Then one day, I suddenly stopped and thought, "Hang on, at what point do they start joining in and this become a sharing thing?" '

After several years of taking their children's needs into account, many parents naturally expect their children to start returning the favour. They look forward to being treated with equal care and consideration and having some help around the house.

*'I must say, I thought it would be a nice easy gradual changeover from me taking care of their every need, as newborn babies, when what they want is what they need, to them taking more and more care of themselves . . . and me as well!'*

This mother is slowly coming to the realization that she has made everything too comfortable for her children for too long for them now to question how *she* feels. Most parents find out the hard way that children who are used to having everything done for them, who have not been encouraged to think of their parents as anything beyond feeding and cleaning machines, are unlikely to question the status quo.

*'The other day my ten-year-old daughter asked me to do something for her and I said in a cross way, "I'm not your servant" and she looked at me with genuine amazement, and said, "I thought you were."'*

Parents often meet our suggestions that children participate more in the life of the family with 'Yes, that's all very well, I've tried, but my children continue to expect me to do everything for them.' We point out that that is only to be expected. After all, they've never known it any other way! Parents who start by doing everything for their children, and let that everything just get bigger and bigger, fail to renegotiate areas of responsibility. Luckily, it's never too late to renegotiate. Starting early, even if our children are too little to help us in any major way, helps them to see us as people too.

*'Since Miles was born, I've been totally immersed — looking after him, feeding him, being with him. It's only in the last few months that he's now at nursery that I've been able to go out and do things. I've joined a pottery class for instance. The other day, I was talking to him about my pottery and he was interested — seeing something else in mum, someone that wasn't just there for him but had another life as well.'*

Letting our children know we'd like their help and support encourages them to become more receptive and considerate. It educates them to become aware of the needs of others and helps guard against the sort of 'learned helplessness' that causes such conflict between parents and their older teenage children later on.

Before we can let our children know we'd like their help, however, we have to let go of being Supermum or Superdad — tireless, infallible, with endless reserves of energy, enthusiasm and patience. We have to dare to let our children see us as we are: human, tired, occasionally worn right out. We have to let them see that we have needs and concerns just like they do, that sometimes we don't know all the answers or that we can be wrong.

'Children take what they are given', says Pat Slade. 'They can't say, or be expected to say, "Hang on, mum, what about you?" She learned the hard way. 'Because my mother never had much time for me, I was always determined that I was going to be there for my children one hundred per cent of the time. And the result was that I got burned out because I wasn't looking after myself at all.' She felt resentful towards her children for all her non-stop mothering until she came to the groups and realized that they could not be blamed for how she felt: they didn't even know how she felt. She had never told them.

Many parents, like Pat, feel they shouldn't let their children know how they are feeling. They worry about overburdening them, destroying childhood as an idyll of happiness and innocence where no one is seriously hurt and all is well with the world. They feel their children should be 'protected' from the expression of 'negative' feelings, such as loneliness, sadness or uncertainty.

A useful guideline here would seem to be one of balance: while it's obviously inappropriate to burden children with every detail of our own problems and insecurities, it may be just as unwise and unhelpful to exclude them from the day-to-day emotions that we are feeling.

*"Suddenly, when I was about fifteen, my mother cried for the first time and I realized that she was unhappy with my father. I thought she must be crying all the time, that that was her whole life, and it was the first time she'd considered me old enough to hear it.'*

Small children are particularly adept at picking up the unspoken messages around them. Struggling to keep our feelings to ourselves means they can only guess at half of what is going on. With their easy tendency to take responsibility onto themselves for what happens inside the family, their guesses may have profound influences on how they feel about themselves and the way they interpret the situations around them.

*'I can see now how maybe Grant had come to build a barrier between us. At one point during the painful breakup of my marriage, I announced "I don't want the children" — in front of them. If only I could have told them why I didn't feel strong enough to have them with me, that it was because of me and not a reflection on them.'*

'We feel we have to do everything for them and it starts off because we want to do everything for them. We want to do what we think is right and best and show that we love them and we wear ourselves out.'

As parents, putting our own needs first occasionally goes right against the grain. How often do you hear parents say things like 'I just decided to take ten minutes for myself'? Parents, mothers especially, aren't supposed to do things for their own pleasure and definitely aren't expected to put themselves first; they come right at the end of the list after children, partner, granny, where there is one — even the family guinea pig. Most of the parents we see go along with this line of priorities because they feel that looking after themselves better can only be achieved at some cost to their children. They think that the price of being happier, more fulfilled individuals is that of being neglectful 'bad' parents when, actually, within reasonable limits, the reverse is true. Children do not want to have self-pitying martyrs for parents.

Mary Amersham had been preparing a traditional Sunday roast for a friend who was visiting from abroad, complete with all the trimmings. Her daughter, Ann, had hired a video the day before. 'On Sunday morning she said to my ex-husband who'd been invited to this lunch as well, "Oh, come upstairs and watch this video." So everyone was upstairs watching the video and I was slaving away in the kitchen doing this splendid Sunday lunch. We finally sat down with beautifully starched pink napkins. The meal was delicious. I had excelled myself. But I was pretty silent throughout the meal. And there came a stage when Ann said "Mum, I'd rather sit down to bread and jam and a happy mother than have this beautiful meal and you feeling resentful." And I said, "You are right. I am feeling resentful. How did you know?" And she pulled this wonderful face and said "You've been smiling but your mouth has been going fsfsfs." '

If, like Mary, we are constantly pushing down our own needs whenever they threaten to emerge, they won't just go away. They'll remain just beneath the surface, endlessly awaiting settlement. Sometimes they may emerge in disguise.

*'My mother was totally giving. It was only later I realized that she took attention for herself by being ill. She was always suffer-*

*ing with her heart and her nerves and taking pills and needing a doctor. It was her only way of saying she needed someone to look after her, to think about her for a change. It was only when we all left home that she became fit and healthy.'*

Sometimes our unfulfilled needs can emerge in more problematic ways to affect the lives of our children, as we put pressure on them to be everything that we are not, dumping our unfulfilled dreams and second hand ambitions on them, demanding perhaps that they continue in our chosen careers or urging them to succeed where we failed, often in fields quite unsuited to their particular talents.

An important American study, carried out by Burton White, has shown that when it comes to bringing up healthy, creative and self-assured young people, what really matters is how their parents feel about themselves. How much time and money they spend on their children or what school they send them to or even what 'parenting' philosophy they adhere to, is not as important. He found that parents who felt good about themselves and communicated that to their children, gave them one of the best examples that they could.

*'I knew I wanted my children to grow up independent and self-reliant, not aggressive but able to go out and get what they wanted, but I never realized the example had to be me, that the most powerful way of influencing them was to be the sort of person that I wanted them to be.'*

Children live what they learn and they learn by imitation. As parents, we are the people they imitate more closely than anyone else. Our own everyday experience tells us how our children act like the most unmerciful mirror, picking up our most unguarded gestures and slips of speech, parading out statements that, to our embarassment, we recognize as our own!

Children learn from us how to *be* in the world — and they learn this mainly by seeing *how* we behave not by listening to what we *say*. They pick up those aspects of ourselves that make the deepest impression, not necessarily the ones we would select for them. If we want our children to learn certain qualities — trust, confidence, persistence, self-discipline and concentration — and to behave in certain ways — not swearing, not smoking — the most effective way of doing so is by acting them out so that they, in turn, will copy them.

*'It was a tremendous relief to realize that instead of smacking my children, which never had*

*any kind of good effect on them or me, I could have a better effect by not smacking them, because then I could really say to them, "It's not nice to hit each other." '*

If, as this mother discovered, we are always pushing our children to be a certain way and then acting the opposite, exhorting them to be truthful in all circumstances and then shouting 'Tell him, I'm out'

when an unwanted caller comes to the door, they will usually follow our real rather than our spoken lead. Example is much more powerful than instruction.

*'My Mum was always saying, "Why can't you tidy up?" And you only had to go into her study and find it littered with papers. She never did what she was always trying to get us to do.'*

'I used to resent playing with my children because I thought I had better things to be doing with my time. Now I get involved in their play in ways I used to enjoy as a child, that way I am doing it for me as well as them and everything feels a whole lot better.'

Many of the parents we meet would probably benefit from being 'guilty' of looking after themselves better, paying more attention to their own needs. People who give out continually without getting anything back for themselves soon become unable to give out at all.

We have been struck by how hard some people find it to start taking care of themselves and to consider their own needs of any real importance. When we question them, we find that these tend to be people who were taught as children that their own needs

didn't count, that it was more important to behave correctly rather than go for what they wanted, that their point of view was unimportant and not worth listening to. It's precisely because these feelings linger, often for a lifetime, that we need to encourage our children to feel worthwhile and of value from as early an age as possible.

In the meantime, a good way to start bolstering our own self-esteem and attending to our own needs is to use some of our nurturing skills on ourselves. At times,

## What am I doing for me?

Take a piece of paper and write down your ten favourite activities, things you really like to do just for yourself and would do even, or perhaps especially, if you didn't have a family. They may include going out to the cinema, walking in the country, reading adventure novels or flicking through magazines. Mark beside each one how often you do them. For example:
O = often, S = sometimes, H = hardly ever, N = never.

_____

_____

_____

_____

_____

_____

_____

_____

_____

_____

As you work through this exercise, be aware of what you would like to do differently or do more of. How could you make this possible?

One woman made the following comments on doing this exercise:

_'At first I found this really difficult. Everything I thought of was to do with doing something for somebody else. Then I went back to a time before I had the children, before I was married, and all these things came flooding back to me. Dancing, I loved dancing, and walking on cliffs by the sea and being by myself ... It was really quite a relief to find out that I did know what I liked to do after all. Now all I need is the courage to start doing them again.'_

this is really not so very different from caring for our children.

*'I am becoming more and more aware that inside me there is a little child that needs looking after, giving attention to and having a good time. Part of the reason I don't feel good at times is because this little inner me is being left out.'*

At our parent support groups, parents are encouraged to become aware of this inner child — the part of themselves that never got valued or taken seriously or treated as special when they were young — and to give it some long overdue attention and care. Although caring for ourselves can be hard to fit in with caring for the children and the rest of the household, sometimes it can coincide with it.

*'I had always been told I couldn't paint, I'd never be an artist, so I might as well give up. That was at age seven! Now, my children love to paint at home, I join them doing it just like the seven-year-old artist I was prevented from being. It's great! I'm not there to help them or supervise or do it right, just to explore like they do and have fun!'*

Many, many parents notice an immediate improvement in their relationships with their children when they start to give themselves some time and attention. They discover it's in *everyone's* interests that they look after themselves.

*'One day when my daughter was a baby, I sent her off to a baby-sitter and I went swimming, went to the hairdresser and then met my husband for lunch. And I remember, when I went to pick her up, I actually felt I'd been away for days rather than just a few hours, as though I'd been away on holiday. And the nice thing was that I was very happy to pick her up. It felt good to get back again.'*

## 'Sometimes I feel so connected to them I'm not sure where I end and they begin.'

As parents, our lives are so bound up with those of our children that it can sometimes seem we are one and the same person: we hurt for them, thrill for them, bristle with anger on their behalf, share their triumphs, lament their woes. Often we get so practised at thinking 'for' our children, anticipating every need and then seeing that it's met, that we continue supervising their lives and sorting out their problems long after it's appropriate to do so.

'When a child is really upset, everything inside me boils to do something', says Joan, summing up how every parent feels. It took her a while to see that although coming up with answers to her children's problems may have been useful in the short-term, in the long-term it actually went right against her professed goal of helping them grow up resourceful and self-reliant, confident in their ability to handle the problems they came up against.

Children who get accustomed to having their parents come up with the answers tend to become dependent on them as fixers and solvers. In our experience, it's not so much laziness that's to blame as lack of confidence.

Nearly all children greatly overestimate how knowledgeable and wise their parents are and belittle their own abilities. But some parents unwittingly encourage these attitudes by intervening and taking over, always being on hand to 'help'. Their children, getting little practice in sorting out the problems of day-to-day living for themselves, tend to become even more dependent, increasingly stuck in the rut of having their lives directed for them and their problems solved by proxy. Or they have to assert their independence by wrenching themselves away from the hand that helps them.

*'My father was always very concerned about me. And the result was that I actually stopped talking to him about what was going on in my life, certainly about any problems I was having, for about five years. I needed to talk but I didn't want his advice, particularly when it was right because then I had to go and do something else so I could be sure it was me deciding and not him!'*

How do we get to know when it is appropriate to be fixers and solvers and when not? When to give advice and when not? When to get indignant on our children's behalf and step in and when to sit back and let them work things out for themselves? One way to know what is appropriate when is to ask ourselves whose need is not being met? Figuring out whose need is not being met rather than jumping in to solve the problem will allow us to help in the most useful way.

## Whose problem is it anyway?

Here are some typical family scenarios, study them, asking your-self the question 'whose need is not being met?', and see if thereby you can work out who owns the problem. Match your conclusions with those at the end of this chapter

- Your child comes home from school upset about the way a friend has acted towards him

- Your child can't find his football boots

- Your child is playing in front of the television getting in the way of you watching it

- Your child's room is so untidy you can't get in to clean it

- Your child is drawing pictures on your best table

- You are worried because your child complains he is being bullied at school

- You get angry when your eldest child teases the youngest one to a point where he gets upset

- Your child wants to make a camp in the kitchen and you want the kitchen clear to so you can cook the supper

It's obviously unrealistic to suppose we can, or even should, be totally objective in our dealings with our children in the style of a professional helper or counsellor — as parents, we cannot help but be involved in what happens in their lives. Nevertheless, if we get emotionally caught up in their problems all our energy and attention can go into the feelings *we're* having rather than helping them to deal with their own emotions. Not surprisingly, children can find this an additional burden. No child wants to feel responsible for how another adult is feeling — especially when it's her own parent.

*'I could never tell my Father any-thing, although he was always terribly keen to hear, because he would get so upset about it. And then I would have the problem I had started off with, bullying in the playground or whatever, plus the problem of his upset-ness ... My Mother generally didn't listen and if she did would*

*offer reassuring comments. I soon stopped discussing any of my problems with them and I still don't.'*

---

## Other people's problems

Spend a couple of days just observing people who are having problems of some sort — in the supermarket, on buses, in your own family . . . Ask yourself who owns the problem. Is somebody taking it on who doesn't need to? Just notice what is happening without trying to change anything that you see.

---

Sometimes of course, the answers are not clear cut. Like any other close relationship, parenthood is a long chapter of conflicting needs: our children want to stay up late and we crave peace and quiet; they want loud music on the hi-fi and we would like something more melodic; they leave things lying around while we desire order. Although ways of dealing with these conflicts are explored in Chapter 6, most often we will be able to trace problems back to their owners (us or them) by asking whose need is not being met.

Even when we establish that it's the child's problem because her needs are being interfered with, it's not easy to stand back and distance ourselves. But, with time, our practice and self-control will be rewarded by children who are increasingly self-reliant, confident in their ability both to look after themselves and to sort out most of their own scraps and problems.

The difference for parents, as well as children, can be extraordinary.

*'I've found it an absolute liberation not to jump in, an amazing easing of the burden of being a parent. I find parenting, anyway, the most difficult and demanding job that anybody could ever do — there are times when I think it's just too hard — but if you have to take responsibility for everyone else's problems all the time, it's a superhuman goal. You just can't do it.'*

Even very young children are capable of understanding that their problems are their responsibility.

*'Our three-year-old couldn't find something and it upset her very much. She started screaming. My wife explained that as she had put it away, she ought to know where it was. And she took it in and started looking and found it for herself.'*

Parents worry that withdrawing their 'help' will seem like they are abandoning their children just when they are needed most. Angie Clough's son Peter used to play with the boy next door who was three or four years older. 'I never liked him', said Angie,'He seemed to bring out a side of Peter that I wasn't used to. Peter was very much in awe of him and really rather frightened of him. He would follow him round and literally do everything this lad told him to.

'Peter was aware that I didn't like him and he often used to hide behind me and say "Can you go to the door, Mum, and tell him I don't want to play?" And of course I'd do it. Then one day, they swapped guns for the night. And this lad came back the next day and he had broken Peter's gun. He didn't even say he was sorry. He just sort of threw it down and said, "It's broken." I was really fuming, but I managed to tell myself, and keep on telling myself, "It's nothing to do with me. It's Peter's problem."

'The lad came back two or three times, wanting his own gun back, and Peter still tried to get me to go to the door. But I said, "No, it's your problem, it's not my problem, you sort it out." It was about the hardest thing I've ever had to do. And for a week Peter kept that lad waiting for his own gun and, in the end, he came back and actually apologized, which was unheard of. From then on Peter seemed to be much more confident in the way he handled this child. It gave him an assertiveness that wasn't there before.'

Before, when Angie used to take Peter's problems on, he would often blame her when the solution didn't work out as he had hoped; after all, it was *her* solution. Now he has to live with the consequences of his own decisions, it's taking some getting used to. Sometimes he still says helplessly, 'Why can't you just tell me what to do?' but he's gradually getting to accept that she's not going to get drawn in.

And, as a result of having to deal with his problems himself, he's gaining confidence.

Fifteen-year-old Christine Yates often does her homework very late at night. Her mother's instinct is to say, 'You must go to bed early, put the light off in good time, so that you are fresh to get up and go to school tomorrow', but, since coming to the groups, she's started letting Christine sort it out for herself. 'I realized I was still thinking of myself as the parent putting her child to bed. I thought I was acting in her best interests, protecting her from being too tired to get up the next morning. But I had to rethink, I was *forced* to rethink. Otherwise I would have continued functioning as though she were still about ten.'

Christine appreciates the difference: 'Because you aren't saying anything about stopping', she told her mother, 'I do stop because I know that it's me that is being affected. If I stay up too long, I think "Oh God I'm not going to do that again" because I felt really awful the next day. But working till eleven or so isn't that late for me. I can take it.'

The non-interference principle continues to apply when children have problems and arguments between themselves. When Marjorie Bell's two sons squabbled and fought, she always felt she had to rush in, taking it upon herself to sort out who was right and who was wrong, always trying scrupulously to be 'fair'. Then she found that if she could stand back and be more detached initially, she didn't get embroiled.

'I learned that way how incredibly important it is for me to let the children sort out their own squabbles. It's my involvement in their squabbling that disturbs my equilibrium. Now I either tend to extricate myself completely, which I would have never been able to do before. Or, if it's getting really rough and violent, I'll say "Let's sit down and talk about it." But I make it clear that it's their problem and it's still up to them, therefore, to come up with an answer. I'm just there to help them.'

She can't believe the difference this simple process of detachment has made. 'Since I stopped adjudicating and intervening and listening to see who had right on his side and who didn't, they've kind of given up on me and tend to sort it out themselves anyway.'

June Hargreaves found she was not only taking on her four-year-old's problems, but the problems she assumed other people were having as a consequence of how he was behaving. For a year she resisted taking him to London because travelling on the underground with him was such an ordeal. 'He would stand on the seat and climb about and then jump onto the floor.

And I felt everybody looking at me and expecting me to do something — tell him off or smack him or something. So I'd make token gestures, saying feebly, "Oh, Johnny don't", so they'd know it wasn't my fault, that I had acknowledged their displeasure and was trying to do something about it. He of course took not the slightest bit of notice and carried right on with his game.'

With the help of the group, June came to realize that she was taking on what she assumed were their problems with his behaviour when neither she nor her son had any kind of problem with the situation: 'I didn't care whether he jumped on the seats or not, so long as he was happy and not interfering with the other people or being aggressive. It doesn't worry me if he uses his surroundings for his entertainment. If it worries other people they must sort it out with him. I also found that a lot of the 'disapproval' I was picking up was pure fantasy. They didn't even notice most of the time, and I'm sure they would anyway much rather he was amusing himself than crying.'

It might be that another parent in a similar situation feels so uncomfortable with her child's behaviour that she has to do something about it:

*'I knew from talking it through in the group that Sammy's behaviour towards other adults when we visited friends was actually their problem not mine. Yet, I felt so dreadful if I sat back and left them to do something about it, I ended up deciding that I had a real problem too and, as my problem was actually worse than anyone's I had to deal with it first.'*

'I don't want to take on this thing of the homework. I'd love it if Roger would take it over! But then Roger somehow doesn't seem to do it, or does it really late at night and I feel responsible.'

Inevitably, all parents have real dilemmas about subjects that ostensibly lie in the child's domain. It is hard for many parents to avoid getting involved in homework, for example, and to leave it to their children to sort out. Most of us have been brought up to consider completing school set work as critically important to our eventual success in school and thereby probably in job applications and life in general. Yet, of course, few children below school-leaving age can grasp the long-term considerations about school success — the future to them is a week away not what might, or might not, happen at the age of twenty.

Issues such as these can only be decided on an individual basis. One family may come down in favour of a firm set of rules and enforce them, whilst another may accept totally that homework is the child's issue and leave it to them completely. A middle way is possible for many.

*'Freddie does his own homework at the moment. I don't know how well he does it, but I feel that's something he has to sort out with his teachers. If he's not doing it well enough, they will confront him about it. Although we don't supervise him or say "That's not done well enough, do it again", we have let him know that we expect him to take care of his homework. And when he does take himself off at six to do it, as he has said he will, we reinforce it, "That's great, you've kept to your intentions of doing your homework."'*

This example illustrates that, even as we extricate ourselves from our children's problems, we can still find constructive ways of helping them. We don't have to act unconcerned, saying 'It's your problem, go away and solve it.'

So what sort of things can we do? We can *really* listen and attend to what they are telling us for a start (there's more about this in Chapter 4). We can also let them know we have confidence in their abilities by asking 'What do you think *you* could do about it? Any ideas?' and leaving them room enough to tell us, without evaluating each suggestion as though we were some final arbiter or judge. Even when directly asked for help, we can avoid dictating what they should do. Instead we can offer suggestions with specific examples drawn from our own experience, while all the time letting them know these are only suggestions and the final choice is up to them. We can also invite them to comment on what we suggest and perhaps even to improve upon it.

To begin with, we may find that we are often called upon to come up with ideas. Things may seem no different at all, especially when our children grab at the first thing we suggest and straightaway act on it. Habits are hard to break, for children just as much as grown-ups. If they have got accustomed to having us supply solutions, it will take a while for them to adjust.

*'It wasn't easy at first. They had got so used to being told what to*

*do all the time that I think they genuinely didn't know how to think for themselves. I would have to tease suggestions from them almost painfully with questions like "What do you think George (an older cousin) would do?" At the start I would often have to throw in a few ideas of my own to get them going, taking pains to say something like "If I were in your shoes I might do such and such."'*

This may seem little different from the old way, but there is a difference, because right from the start we are leaving the responsibility with the child, not making up her mind for her and saying "Why don't you do this?" but leaving her to make the final choice and saying, 'Now let's think what we can do about this, have you any ideas?' and letting her come forward with possible solutions before we do.

*'I would be quite firm at times, sending them off to write down all the things they could think of doing on a wet day when they complained of being bored; refusing point blank to come up with the answers.'*

Of course, giving our children more responsibility for finding their own answers to their problems means that we have to trust that they *can* find their answers, even if they need a little help and prompting from us. It is impossible to help people solve their own problems if we believe we are the only ones with the answers.

*'When I first started trying to encourage my children to think of their own answers to little problems, it was very easy to slip back into the old patterns. My son would come up with an idea and I would push it aside saying something like "Oh that will never work" until one day he told me in no uncertain terms that if I never thought his ideas were any good why didn't I just tell him what to do. That brought me up short I can tell you.'*

'Sometimes it's enough just to acknowledge that she needs my attention. If I take half a minute to tell her that I know she wants me to concentrate on her and play her game or stop talking to my friend in the shop; if I get down on one knee and talk to her that way about it, she is usually prepared to be patient for a bit longer.'

Asking whose needs are not being met when problems arise can not only help us identify whose problem is whose but also deepen our understanding of why our children act and react in certain ways.

All behaviour is geared to meet needs. As babies we have relatively simple needs and simple ways of getting them met: we need to eat, sleep, feel warm, be secure and safe, be exposed to a certain amount of stimulation so that we can develop and grow. If we don't get fed or changed or stimulated, we experience discomfort, pain, loneliness, fear or frustration and demand something be done about it by crying.

As we grow up, our needs become more sophisicated as do the ways we have of communicating and meeting them. Toddlers develop needs for being in control of their environment, for independence, for companionship and much more. Eventually a whole range of needs develop from the physical (shelter, warmth, nourishment) and social (companionship, belonging, sexuality) to the emotional and spirital (searching for truth, having a sense of purpose to life.)

---

## Needs

Here are some primary needs that all individuals have. What do your children currently do to meet these needs, or get you to meet them for them?

- Need for attention (for example, crawling along the back of visitors on the sofa)

- Need to feel fully part of the family (for example not wanting to go to bed in the evenings)

- Need to develop their own sense of independence (for example saying 'no', even to things they really like, or refusing to go to bed at the times you decide)

- Need for security (for example coming into bed in the middle of the night after a bad dream)

- Need to explore and learn (for example climbing high fences)

- Need to feel useful (for example helping you clean the floor, even if it is with a dirty mop!)

As well as being different at different times, the ways we choose to meet our needs will vary with age too. The two-year-old going through a phase of saying 'no' to absolutely everything, including the things she likes, is struggling to express her separate identity, her need to be independent from her parent; a teenager battling against father or mother over times to come home may be struggling to assert exactly the same need, but expressing it in different, rather more sophisticated, ways.

Although all of us share the same needs, the ways we develop of meeting them vary enormously. Over time, we all develop our unique stratagems for getting what we want. And children are no exception. They choose the particular behaviour that seems to serve them best.

*'My son Alex was always wandering into the kitchen saying he was hungry, when he'd only had a meal half-an-hour ago. We talked about it and it turned out he was bored, didn't know what to do with himself, and his response to that was to come and ask for something to eat.'*

This father sat down with his son and thought of other more effective, long-lasting ways that Alex could amuse himself. Once he became conscious of what he truly needed, he was in a position to make choices which were more constructive — more likely to answer the underlying need.

Although children's needs can be far from obvious, it can be immensely useful at times just to accept that there is a valid need behind their behaviour. Often, it doesn't matter particularly what the actual need is. We don't have to be amateur sleuths or professional psychoanalysts, but it does help enormously to recognize that there is a need there somewhere, especially when a child is behaving in ways we might find irritating, trivial, childish or just plain mystifying. Being aware that she is not being difficult for its own sake, or deliberately rubbing us up the wrong way, can help make life a lot more tolerable!

*'I used to react almost aggressively when Richard clung to my skirts and followed me around. I could only see it from my point of view. Realizing that he was not doing it to annoy me but to fulfil some real need in him allowed me to see it from his point of view as well. I didn't have to know what the reason was, whether he was just bored or lonely or suffering some deeper emotional need — that didn't matter, what did was that I could accept him for trying to get his needs met. It was just the behaviour I didn't like!'*

As this parent discovered, being accepting and loving towards her child, and thereby helping him find other more appropriate ways of meeting his needs, made a big change from getting angry or ignoring him completely — reactions that often only had the effect of redoubling Richard's efforts and making him even more clingy. Quite often, repeatedly 'bad' behaviour is a recurring attempt to meet the same unfulfilled need. Although the behaviour may get punished, the underlying need often goes unmet.

One of the needs we come up against most often with our children is the need all young people (and old ones too, for that matter!) have to feel loved, accepted, part of what is important in life and generally approved of. To satisfy this need, children require lots of contact with those closest to them. Many parents discount their children's behaviour by saying 'Oh they are only after attention' when this is actually a perfectly valid need, and a very important one — so important, in fact, that children will struggle to receive even unpleasant attention rather than make do with none at all.

We have all watched children in public places struggling to get their parents' attention. They come and show them something and get shooed away; they ask a question and are brushed aside; eventually, more often than not, they do something 'bad' or 'naughty' that the parent cannot afford to ignore and in that way get a few moments of very concentrated attention. Even as they wilt under the harshness of an angry parent's response, it is possible to see the relief on the face that says, 'Well, at least they care enough about me to get angry.'

*'I can always tell when I have been ignoring the boys for too long; they will get up to what my mothers calls mischief, drawing on the papers, which they know their father hates them doing, or fighting with each other, which they know I hate. In the old days I would just get livid with them, but now I know there is a good reason for the behaviour, however much I dislike it, I can intervene and help them find something more constructive to do — without getting angry in the process.'*

Unfortunately many children don't learn to get love and attention by being healthy, happy, curious and energetic but by being ill, hurt, sad, unhappy or disruptive.

*'When I first started to teach I found it very difficult to give positive attention to some of the difficult children that I had in my class. I was either having to deal with them because they were disrupting the other*

*children or I was leaving them alone, because, thank goodness, right at that moment they were quiet and my fear was that I* *would "start them off again" if I disturbed them. In effect I was ignoring them when they were doing the very thing I wanted!*

## Getting attention

What did you do as a child that guaranteed getting some attention, good or bad, from your mother, father, other members of your family, teachers or friends?

## Whose problem was it anyway?

In the first two instances mentioned earlier (page 56), the problem belongs to your child: *He* is upset about his friend, *he* can't find his football boots; you have not had the horrible time in the playground; you are not upset or inconvenienced. You may hate to see him upset, and long to help, but it is — at least initially — his problem.

In the next three instances, the problem belongs to you: your child is quite happy with the situation you are not; it's your TV watching that is being disrupted, not his game; your best table that is being progressively devalued with each new squiggle; your standards of tidiness that are being affronted every time you walk into his bedroom.

The last three examples mentioned are less clear cut. When you get upset about your child being bullied, you are already beginning to share his problem. In these cases, you may need to deal with your own feelings before you are in a situation to help him.

## Summary

- Newborn babies depend on us to meet all their needs; eighteen-year-olds are (theoretically) entirely independent. The challenge for us, as parents, is to help our children become self-reliant and to take on responsibilities as they are capable.

- Our role as a parent changes over time. Sometimes we continue in one role long after it's time to move on to the next. Can we give our children more responsibility for certain parts of their lives?

- Handing over more responsibility, even for small things, gives valuable practice for later life.

- If, as our children grow, we also ask that they become more sensitive to our needs, we will be educating them to become more receptive and considerate to the needs of others generally.

- To do this, we need to let them know what our needs are *and* to be seen to give our needs some priority.

- Taking care of ourselves and, within reason, getting what we want furnishes our children with a great example for the future and helps ensure that we don't dump our own unfulfilled dreams and ambitions on them.

- We get so practised at looking after our children's needs and solving their problems that we may not be giving them a chance to solve their problems for themselves. This can undermine their confidence in their ability to sort things out for themselves.

- We can identify whose problem is whose by asking 'Whose needs are not being met?' and giving the person whose needs aren't being met the chance to solve the problem themselves.

- When our children are squabbling between themselves, we don't have to get involved as referees or umpires.

- There are ways of helping our children solve their problems without taking the problem on and solving it for them. These are expanded upon in Chapters 4 and 6.

- Thinking about needs helps us gain new understanding of our children's behaviour, especially the most unacceptable variety!

- Looking beyond the behaviour to the need gives us new insights into the need and alternative ways of dealing with the behaviour.

# CHAPTER 3

# COMMUNICATION

'When Jane was about four, I just realized that things were happening that I didn't want. We were going wrong. The whole relationship just felt wrong.'

Lack of communication is one of the most common dissatisfactions of family life. Parents complain that they can't get through to their children. Children say their parents never listen. And it's not the generation gap that's at fault. Couples say with sadness that they never talk together any more.

This growing failure to communicate, even with our nearest and dearest, was highlighted by an American survey of several hundred couples whose conversations were recorded over several weeks using voice-activated tape recorders. The results showed that when the odd exchange, such as 'pass the salt', was omitted, couples conversed on average for just twenty-seven and a half minutes *a week*.

People come to our parent support groups for lots of different reasons, but mainly because they hope to find happier, more effective ways of communicating with their children. They not only want their children to feel able to confide in them but would also like to be able to tell them how they feel about the not-so-good parts of family life without a major row developing, with doors slamming and nobody speaking to each other for a week.

These parents are looking for alternatives — other ways of responding that will give better results than the ones they are currently getting. 'The old ways do not work', said one parent quite simply. 'The nagging and shouting, yelling and pleading, are getting us nowhere and wearing us out. We need something to put in their place.'

Our aim is to give people a *choice*, to help them find other possible ways of responding that can then lead to alternative outcomes. Parents find this especially valuable if they have got stuck in particular patterns of acting and reacting. While they may know that these patterns are not having the results they'd like, they keep repeating them for lack of anything to replace them with.

Getting rid of our old unuseful patterns is certainly easier once we have something to exchange them for, but it's still a long, hard process. While children readily adapt to the new, adults find it more difficult. Changing lifelong habits takes commitment, motivation, lots of practice and support.

*'As I practise, I find that I'm gradually changing the ratio of useful to unuseful things. There are still times, of course, when I'm fed up and I can't give to them or listen to them. I still shout at my children occasionally and lose my temper, especially when I feel miserable. I can't always be loving and accepting and all those things; it's not possible.'*

'The ideals were not new to me at all. I had always wanted these things for my children and thought we should have more equal relationships but it was through the skills that these ideals became more accessible, more of a possibility. They represented the way forward I'd been looking for.'

The academic debate about the relative importance of nature and nurture — whether children are born or made — still rages. There are, of course, many factors outside our control and we would be wise to accept them. As every new parent quickly realizes when they hold their first-born in their arms, babies arrive with very definite personalities and wills of their own. Nevertheless, as parents, we know intuitively that there is much we can do to enrich and encourage our children's development; much, too, of course that we can do to thwart or diminish it. It's not that we set out to make our children fail or feel inadequate. Our mistakes are mainly inadvertent.

Developing our ability to communicate enables us to be reasonably sure that we are putting across the sort of messages we want our children to receive. There's nothing mysterious about the concept of communication skills. They are not invented by academics with long lists of letters after their names, but are taken from real life, being based on careful observation of people who naturally communicate well and clearly get results.

We've all met them: corner shopkeepers and local vicars, doctors, hairdressers and other 'ordinary' people who have come to be known as good listeners. These are the people who let us know that they care about what we have to say and with whom we feel safe enough to unburden ourselves. They help us work through our thoughts, worries and fears in ways that make us feel we've found the answers for ourselves. They manage to make themselves heard and understood without getting upset or aggressive or causing others to become so. They 'mean what they say and say what they mean' without hurting other people, handling difficult situations in calm and diplomatic ways, helping to resolve things for the benefit of all concerned.

It's perhaps because we are borrowing these skills from life that they don't seem, even on first acquaintance, so much taught techniques as straightforward common sense. It seems quite obvious that if we listen to people and accept what they tell us, rather than butting in with our own point of view or contradicting what they say, they will feel safe enough to trust us with further confidences. *Of course*, raising our voice and shouting at people makes them feel defensive and even less inclined to help us. That's how we feel when people shout at *us*.

The skills may be common sense, but they are not commonly practised. It is one of the ironies of modern life that, as technology and science have advanced by great leaps and bounds, enabling us to extend global communications in a way that would have been unimaginable half a century ago, our ability to communicate with each other on a personal level has diminished. We can bounce messages off satellites, communicate through computers, dial direct to the other side of the world . . . yet we can't talk to our own children, to our friends and colleagues without fear of being misunderstood or giving offence.

The process we go through in our parent support groups of developing practical communication skills is not like starting from scratch with something totally new. Rather it builds on basic abilities that we will have all developed over the years. Even tiny children have ways of communicating that let their parents know in no uncertain way exactly what their needs are. As they grow older and become more articulate, so a huge potential for getting more complicated messages across opens up.

Sometimes, however, the basic early skills get set into patterns and do not continue to evolve and develop. The stamped foot of a temper tantrum as a toddler can still be apparent in a failure to negotiate effectively as an older child or grown-up. The groups give parents the chance to reassess some of the ways they communicate and so develop their basic skills to a more useful working level.

Of course, it would be foolish to pretend that communication is only a matter of skill. More important than any techniques we can learn are qualities such as sincerity and honesty. What we do and what we say pales beside who we *are*.

It's attitudes of acceptance, trust, respect, openness and honesty — what is often referred to as 'empathy' — that are really important. Without them, all the practical skills in the world would just result in manipulation and control, leading to resentment and ultimately a breakdown in communication all over again.

Using these skills may increase the likelihood of our getting more positive co-operative responses from our children but they don't guarantee a good result. Children aren't automatons but individuals. The new approaches may be met with fewer tears and sulks and defiance but they won't 'work' one hundred per cent of the time. Nothing does. Even when we're doing it 'right' we may not get the 'right' response. This can be off-putting to begin with, but with practice, we will soon get to learn what works and what doesn't with our own particular child; what irritates and what soothes him, what distances and what brings closer.

'When we thought about it we found we never were consistent anyway! So it was a relief not to have to worry about it. It certainly improved our own relationship: being allowed to be far apart on some issues actually brought us together.'

Inevitably as we struggle to change, we will come up against some hard-and-fast attitudes about how our children should be brought up — not just on the part of friends, relatives and well-meaning strangers but also within ourselves. Sometimes these attitudes are so deeply entrenched we don't even know we hold them. One of the best examples of this is the idea that we must always be consistent with our children and in complete accord with our partner, whether over really big issues, such as education, or much smaller and more trivial ones. Many parents tie themselves in knots trying to be consistent, often to no one's great advantage.

*Child:* 'Mum, can I have an ice-cream?'
*Mother:* 'Go and ask your Dad.'
*Child:* 'Dad, can I have an ice-cream?'
*Father:* 'Go and ask your Mum.'
*Child:* 'But I have just asked her and she told me to ask you.'
*Father:* 'Well tell her that I told you to ask her.'
*Child:* 'Mum, Dad's just told me to tell you that you've got to tell me if I can have an ice-cream.'
*Mother:* 'Oh well I suppose you can, but go and ask your Dad for 10p.'
*Child:* 'Dad, can I have 10p for an ice-cream.'
*Father:* 'I haven't got 10p.'
*Child:* 'Oh come on, Dad, you haven't looked yet and, oh hurry the van will go soon . . .'
*Father:* 'Let's have a look then, ah there you are.'
*Child:* 'Thanks Dad, OHH!'
*Father:* 'What's the matter now?'
*Child:* 'The van's gone.'

Sources of conflict about bringing up children, inevitable in almost every partnership, tend to be exacerbated now that the territories between the partners have become less clear cut, and the old distinctions between the mother's traditional nurturing role and the father's traditional disciplining role have overlapped. Even more tension-arousing, however, is the feeling that parents should agree about everything — backing each other up, speaking with one voice, presenting a 'united front'. Somewhere, somehow, the potent and dangerous idea has crept into our parenting mythology that 'good' parents are always of a like mind, never disagreeing or 'contradicting' the other. It's extraordinary, too, the lengths some parents will go to to sustain that myth.

*'My parents used to deny that they were ever fighting, ever arguing. They would say, "We're not arguing, we're just discussing such and such." I remember one time my mother threw a saucepan at my father's head and still turned round and told us, "We're just discussing something!" '*

Our own conversations with

children have revealed that they do not set as much store by consistency as we tend to. When their parents present a united front, it can seem uncomfortably like they are ganging up on them.

*'I can always tell when Mum is lying — she says its really important to go to bed early, but I know that's only because Dad thinks so. It's so unfair of her to take his side all the time.' (A ten year old)*

Couples who have learned to live with quite widely varying standards of what to them is acceptable or unacceptable find their children are quite able to understand that people are not always of a like mind. After all, they and their friends certainly aren't. . .

*'My children had to grow up being very flexible. We had two granny flats in the house. One granny was very Victorian, stern and strict. The other was very liberal. In her eyes they could do no wrong. The children accepted these different attitudes quite easily and simply adapted their behaviour according to the flat they were in.'*

*'I know from John's teacher that he behaves in ways in class that we would never tolerate, yet we never see any sign of it at home. He certainly knows how to switch between home and school without any problem!'*

Aiming to be consistent on every occasion can be a big problem for parents as well as children because circumstances are always changing: yesterday we had plenty of time, today we have a headache and a very tight schedule so are we supposed to stick by what was permissible then? In our experience, parents who try to stick to the rules through thick or thin tend to say 'no' far more often than they'd like just in case it sets a precedent of having to say 'yes' ever afterwards.

*'My father was utterly rigid. If he said "no" you couldn't see him wanting to go back on it. You could argue with him and you could see him thinking, "No, I've said no and no it has to be." He was frightened of losing face.'*

We have all seen children asking for sweets over and over again even as one or other parent says 'no'. This is because they detect the ambivalence, the fact that part of mum means it and part doesn't, so the child goes on pressing until finally mum loses her patience and makes her mind up one way or the other, either saying 'no' in such a firm, final way that it's quite clear the subject is closed or relenting, 'OK, but just this once.'

'In general, I tend to say "no"

the subject is closed or relenting, 'OK, but just this once.'

'In general, I tend to say "no" first,' said Mitra, single mother of two small boys, "and then I think about it and maybe change my mind. If I say "Yes" I can't go back on it.' Mitra eventually solved her dilemma by asking her children to give her a minute or two while she thought about it. She then made up her mind and either gave a definite 'yes' or a definite 'no'. When she said 'no' and really meant it, she found that her children would accept it much more easily because they recognized it as an absolute no rather than a provisional one.

Parents who adhere to rigid rules know only too well that children are sticklers for pointing out that they have broken their own rule and forcing them to stick to it. If we treat them rigidly they will certainly see to it that the rules operate just as rigidly in their favour – putting pressure on us to apply them in areas where it is very difficult to do so – 'He can do it, why can't I?'

Feeling we have to be consistent at all costs means that sometimes we will have to cover up what we feel to be permissible in order to allow or enforce the opposite: suddenly we can find ourselves imposing all sorts of rules we do not fully agree with.

*'In some moment of frustration I decided that the children couldn't use my typewriter and, of course, having made the rule I was determined to stick to it. Yet each time they asked I could think of all the fun and good learning experiences they might have from banging away on it. I know they knew I didn't really agree with the new rule because of the way they kept on at me about it. I was having to put a lot of effort into trying to hide my mixed feelings.'*

Mixed feelings are inevitable when we try to live our lives by the book. Absolute standards force us to act in ways that don't feel comfortable and can confuse our children. With this in mind, we feel that it's not so much consistency of *reaction* that parents should be concerned about but consistency of *attitude*. If we are always honest with our children about what we find acceptable or unacceptable and give the reasons why, we maintain an underlying consistency far more powerful than the frequent hypocrisy of the traditional approach. And there is the added bonus that children learn to be straight in their turn.

There are times when parents suffering major problems with young children may be advised to go through a period of sticking to

## Consistency v inconsistency

Human beings are by nature inconsistent — changing their minds frequently about what they think, believe and feel. Although we may have some absolute standards — drawing the line at cruelty to animals, playing with knives, the uncontrolled consumption of sweets and crisps and running into the road — the rest of the time there's a surprisingly wide range of what we may find acceptable. Here are just a few of the variables ...

- WHEN — watching a TV programme is perfectly acceptable after tea, but not when it's tea-time and the food is on the table and the family is gathered together

- WHERE — it might give great pleasure to see children out in the garden running around having fun whereas doing so in the living-room might be considered too much of a risk to the furniture

- WHO — waking up two or three times a night is perfectly acceptable when it's our three-month baby wanting to feed but a problem when it's our four or five-year-old

- HOW — music, dance or gym practice may be quite acceptable until they want us to sit and watch for hours at a time

- WHAT — we might encourage our children to make their own selections from the video library yet draw the line when they choose X-rated films

very set guidelines. If children have been living with the uncertainty of extreme mixed messages, coupled with emotional trauma, they can reach an almost uncontrolled state where they (temporarily) need the security of strict rules and enforced discipline. Having broken the negative patterns of behaviour, however, a relaxing of reactions on the part of the family can then take place and a consistent attitude of honesty and loving support recommended.

## Acceptable and unacceptable behaviour

When, or where, would you find the following acceptable:

• Being slapped hard across the face

_____

• Breaking into a house

_____

• Dressing up as a clown?

_____

And unacceptable:

• Being kissed and cuddled

_____

• Being offered money

_____

## 'The worst thing about my five-year-old is how quickly he can reduce me to the level of a five-year-old.'

The problem of patterns, and how to break out of them, is not of course confined to the small minority of families experiencing really severe difficulties in raising their children. We are all creatures of habit, living our lives according to patterns that have been built up in our childhoods or the more recent past.

Much of our behaviour is unconscious: we act and react without so much as a second thought. These split-second reactions can some-times be useful, and even life-saving, such as when we grab a child to prevent him stepping off a kerb into a busy street. But at other times, such as when we 'fly off the handle' when our child does something we don't like, the pattern seems to serve no purpose. We may hate the way we react and spend a lot of energy resolving _never_ to act that way again. But the very next time our five-year-old behaves a certain way, _wham!_ it pushes a button somewhere and, before we

know it, there we are shouting and getting upset, ranting and raving just as irrationally as our children ever do.

*'I'm always shouting at my children, always in a rage. I know what I'm doing, I hate what I'm doing, I can see it doesn't work, but I don't seem able to break it. It happens before I realize it's happening. What I want more than anything else is the choice — about whether I flare up or not. At the moment, it just happens.'*

Being a parent often makes us aware of strong patterns we were quite oblivious to before. Many of us lead very ordered, calm, civilized lives until our children come along, and then it's as if something has snapped inside and we start flying off the handle at the slightest provocation.

---

## Reflex reactions

Cast your mind back over your experiences as a parent. What are the situations that trigger unhelpful responses? They may be small and silly-sounding, such as your child looking into the carrier bags while you are trying to get on with the shopping. Becoming aware of how you react out of past patterns is like lifting the needle off a record: you may still play the record, yet you can begin to have some conscious choice over when and where.

---

When we're in the grip of them, these reactions seem as instantaneous and outside our control as a knee-jerk reflex. This is because they short-circuit our conscious thinking, operating on a much more basic *physiological* level. There's no time to think or to analyse why we're reacting as we are; before we know it, we've hit out with the wounding words we'll regret later, shouted or smacked our child.

We can help ourselves by cutting into the reaction — the act/react loop — and so give ourselves pause for thought. One of the most powerful ways of disrupting the physiological process taking place inside is by changing the pattern of our breathing.

Taking a deep breath and letting it out slowly gives us just a breath-length of time in which to detach ourselves a fraction and ask whether there's a more appropriate way of responding. There's nothing magical about taking a breath but creating a pause gives us a *choice*, the opportunity of reacting in another, perhaps more useful, way.

*'Usually, when I am on the verge of losing my temper I am standing up. I can feel myself growing taller by the minute and getting all tense in my body. Now I have trained myself at that moment just before I explode to take a very big breath and sit down — on the floor if need be. The combination of changing my breathing and my body position makes all the difference.'*

The challenge for this mother now is to catch the reaction at ever earlier and earlier stages, even before she stands up and starts to feel the explosive anger taking over. Other parents find other solutions. For this father, for example, it's coming up with the most unlikely reaction he can think of.

*'When the boys are starting to get into the sort of state guaranteed to brush me up the wrong way, I will try and do something there and then to break it. The more unexpected and unusual my reaction the more effective it tends to be. I'll just stand on my head or stick out my tongue or think of something totally obscure to say.'*

For other parents, physically removing themselves may sometimes be the only solution.

*'This morning Sandra didn't want to get up for school because she stayed up late last night. I felt my blood starting to boil and I thought, "Well there's just no point, I'm not going to get drawn in." I felt like hitting her because she was really being horrible, but in the end I just left her, went downstairs and got on with what I had to do and in the end she just came out of it.'*

# 'If you hit your brother again, I'll smack you.'

Children inherit our patterns of communicating just as surely as our blue eyes, brown hair or musical ear; just as surely as we too inherited them from our parents.

In an interview in *The Sunday Times*, the journalist and novelist Jill Tweedie talked about her relationship with her son Luke: 'When he was eight the school said they thought he was a bit disturbed. So I went to a shrink, a woman, and when she asked what the problem was I said: "He seems rather distressed and doesn't seem to know where we are, what time it is." I went babbling on explaining that he didn't seem to have any idea of time and place. There was a long silence and then she looked at me and said, "It's four o'clock on Tuesday", and I said, "Yes", and she said, "You were meant to be here last Friday at two o'clock." '

Even when we are quite determined that we are not going to repeat the mistakes of the previous generation, we can find ourselves caught out — reacting in the family way, as it were, for lack of any viable alternative.

'We've got into this terrible pattern of shouting at Miles', said Toni Lewis of her three-year-old. 'He hates it, we hate it, we hate ourselves for doing it. We try not to. We say we're not going to, but sometimes it's just too much.'

With the help of her group co-ordinator, Toni found that when she looked back to *her* childhood the worst thing she remembered was her father shouting at her. 'When I raise my voice with Miles, I can just hear my father talking to me, and he's a completely authoritarian army colonel, not like me at all.'

The problem now, as Toni realizes only too clearly, is that unless she does something to change, Miles will inherit the 'shouting gene' in his own turn. 'I can see it happening already', she said. 'He tends to shout at his friends to get what he wants. If, for some reason, they don't want to do what he asks them, he'll shout at them. It sounds horrible to hear this three-year-old shouting. It goes right to the core of me.'

The Lewis family are still struggling with this one, but they have found that awareness of what they are doing can create alternatives. 'One day this week, we were just sliding into the same routine and Miles said, "Don't shout at me." He's said it before but this time I heard what he was saying. So I took a deep breath and let it out. And then I switched to doing the opposite of what I'd been about to do and started *whispering*. And it became a game, so that whatever it was that I wanted him to do, or not to do, became a whisper, almost a matter of life and death.'

In every family, mini dramas are being played out all the time — the scripts as tightly written as any produced for the theatre, with every player having their cues and set lines which are rehearsed day after day until every player knows his part to perfection. If a new player comes on stage, however, and doesn't know his lines, the whole script can be rendered useless. This explains why parents find themselves 'utterly amazed Johnny behaved so well' when someone new is left to deal with the old problem.

*'I was really anxious the first time my mother came to look after the boys whilst we were away. I dreaded her having to cope with all the things they do to play me up. When we got back after the weekend, I kept asking her "didn't they do such and such or so and so?" I found it quite a struggle to accept that they had behaved so differently with us out of the way.'*

When *we* behave differently, the script can also change. 'It's like having new gears to change down into', said one parent. 'This morning something set me off, so I took a deep breath, let it out and instead of reaching the final blow-up I was able to say, "I'm having a tough morning too" and we parted giving each other a hug and saying "See you this afternoon." '

Though a lot of parents come to be painfully aware of their patterns, they are often totally unaware of their origins. Finding out that sometimes the pattern stretches way back through the generations can be quite a revelation.

*'When you have a family it makes you think about the family you came into. Suddenly you're looking at the whole thing from the other perspective. I've noticed inherited patterns coming through. When I say "inherited patterns", I mean things I don't like, problems. At the moment, they end in me. If I can sort them out, the whole family could be healed, because it gives John the chance of not having to take on the same stuff that's been handed down to me from my parents.'*

When we're dealing with patterns, we learn from failure as well as success. Every time we find ourselves back in the grip of the old pattern, we have a new opportunity to learn and, perhaps, to change; to breathe out and try to alter the end-point even if we started out the same old way. Just as the patterns we don't like have been reinforced by repetition, so changes will only take place by repeating the new behaviour we now want in its place.

Children, of course, get into habits too. Nine-year-old Jane Slade, for example, had developed a habit of 'answering back', responding in an abusive way when she didn't like what she heard 'not just to me but to other adults as well and it sounded awful', said Pat. 'I knew I had to do something, so I made a joke about it. The next time she came back at me with some nasty remark, I said "Hang on a moment. Let's pretend you're on video. And now let's stop the video and rewind and see if you can find another way of saying that because I don't like it when you talk to me in that way. I feel upset, especially when you shout. So let's play it again and see if you can keep the volume down and change the words. And you might get a better reaction from me." It worked beautifully. Now, when Jane answers back, all Pat needs to do is to say, '*Stop*, Video!' and it stops her in her tracks.

## 'She'll never amount to anything.'

### Your self-image

Describe yourself. Just stop and take a few moments to think about who *you* are — not where you live or what you do but who you are, your character and personality. Write down words as they come to mind.

Now look at what you've written. As you read through them, can you hear echoes of your parents, partners, friends and teachers talking. How much does your description of 'you' reflect the judgements of others? Does it really sum up who you are?

Our sense of who we are is determined largely by how others define us — siblings, teachers, friends, and principally parents. Yet parents' definitions often reveal more about *their* hopes and ambitions, fears and preoccupations than they do about their children's: 'She's very artistic, aren't you dear?' disguising the hope 'I'd like her to grow up to be an artist' or 'What a good baby!' actually meaning 'Thank goodness, we can sleep through the night now!' For children, however, these labels represent the truth about themselves. If that's what adults with their vast knowledge and experience say they are, then that's what they must be and so they begin to believe they are 'lazy', 'useless', 'bossy', 'stubborn', 'frightened of the dark', 'a shy little thing', 'a real terror', 'just like her mother.'

The world is full of adults living with the labels unthinkingly stuck on them by parents and teachers half a century or more ago, unconsciously programmed by those repetitions echoing down the years, 'You're no good', 'You'll never amount to anything ...' These early messages are so powerful that we tend to pull them out in later life and use them against ourselves. Unfortunately,

negative messages tend to be remembered more clearly than positive ones because they are delivered with more energy, often in fury or frustration, and so have more impact. We know from our own experience that what we think and say to ourselves *matters:* when we tell ourselves that we are fat, stupid and ugly or that we are useless and will never be successful, the messages become like self-fulfilling prophecies: unconsciously we work away at being just that.

*'When I first thought about the effect of using labels, I felt really resentful towards my parents for all the labels they had used on me. I know now that I didn't deserve them. Talking it through in the group helped me realize that my parents had also suffered from being labelled and so inevitably came to label me. They had acted in the best way they knew, believing it was for my benefit. Realizing that really helped me — leaving me free to understand rather than blame.'*

The tendency to label others is just as strong as the tendency to go along with the labels we are given. And we start young — often before the child's personality has had any chance to establish itself and certainly well before his self-esteem is sufficiently strong to shrug the label off as it deserves. By the time a baby is no more than a few months old, we may have already labelled him 'very bright' or 'a slow learner'. Even though this is obviously ludicrous, very early labels can stick. Sometimes, they can even last a lifetime. In their book, *How To Talk So Kids Will Listen and Listen So Kids Will Talk*, Adele Faber and Elaine Mazlish (Avon Books, 1982) give an extreme example of this early labelling:

'I remember the moment when my son, David, was born. Five seconds had gone by and he still hadn't breathed. I was terrified. The nurse slapped him on his back. No response. The tension was excruciating. She said, "He's a stubborn one!" Still no response. A moment later he finally cried — that piercing sound of the newborn. My relief was indescribable. But later on that day, I found myself wondering, "Is he really stubborn?" By the time I brought him home from the hospital, I had the nurse's comment in its place — foolish words from a foolish woman. Imagine putting a label on an infant less than half a minute old!

'And yet every time during the next few years, when he kept on crying no matter how long I patted or rocked him, when he wouldn't try a new food, when he refused to take his nap, when he balked at getting on the bus to nursery school, when he wouldn't wear a sweater on a cold day, the thought would flit through my mind. "She was right. He is stubborn." '

Of course, we do not deliberately set out to make a child stubborn or clumsy or a slow learner, but if we do have these attitudes and expectations, he will find it difficult not to fall in with them. Teachers know quite well that if they go on telling a child he's naughty or disruptive long enough he will become naughty and disruptive in order to satisfy their expectations.

Australian family therapist, Steve Biddulph, calls this unconscious programming 'accidental hypnosis'. 'What most people fail to realize', he writes, 'is that hypnosis is an everyday event. Whenever we use certain patterns of speech, we reach into the unconscious minds of our children and program them, even though we have no such intention.' (*The Secret of Happy Children*, Steve Biddulph, Bay Books, 1985.)

In one study carried out at the University of Michigan, a group of students was randomly divided into two. Their teachers were told that one group had exceptionally high achievement potential while the other was only average. The teachers adapted their methods to these expectations — being more accepting, praising and encouraging of the first group and giving them more of their time, attention and support. This first group rewarded their teachers with markedly higher results than the only-average group about whom the teachers had felt lukewarm and had tended to write off.

## 'Look, Mum! I did up my buttons!'
## 'But you've got your shoes on the wrong feet!'

Just reaching back into our own experience tells us how damaging labels can be — and how hard to shrug off — yet many of us find it hard to stop labelling our children. We feel the only way to bring them up competent, civilized and reasonably well-mannered is to point out what they're doing wrong, to criticize and pick holes. It's a modern version of hellfire and brimstone and cautionary tales: tell them they're bad, and it will make them better.

Far from helping a child improve, however, constantly pointing out what he's doing wrong is more likely to discourage him from believing he can do *anything* right and further reinforce his feelings of hopelessness and failure.

We often believe that if we point out the things our children do wrong, they will correct them, with the result that we can become nit-picking to a fault, always criticizing and commenting on what they do wrong rather than looking for what they get right. In some families, mealtimes, traditionally a time of closeness and harmony, degenerate into those all too familiar running commentaries: 'Don't talk with your mouth full . . . Close your mouth when you chew . . . Finish what's on your plate . . . Hold your fork properly . . . You've got something on your chin . . .' and on and on and on.

For some reason we feel that the good doesn't need commenting on.

*'My husband calls it the "southeastern disease". Like with the summer in England; everybody moans about the weather all the time but when the good weather comes they don't say anything. They wait for it to start raining so they can all start moaning again!'*

When children get things right, even for the first time, many parents take it for granted. Somehow successes don't shriek at them in quite the same way that mistakes do, when the shoes are on the wrong feet, for example, or the buttons are all funny. It's the rare parent who, when their child comes home and tells them he got fifteen out of twenty in a spelling test, emphasizes the fifteen correct ones rather than the five he got wrong.

Sometimes if we ignore the negative and focus on the positive instead, however, our children's self-esteem will be so much increased they may make the changes we are looking for unasked. When a child comes downstairs with his shoes on the wrong way round and proudly announces he's done his buttons up, we could stop to acknowledge,
'You are looking very pleased with yourself. You've done a good job getting dressed. Let's put your shoes on the other feet.'

*'I always thought that for a child to improve, you had to point out what they did wrong. I can see now how we set up our son to fail. I would try and teach him to cook and get so impatient that I criticized him until he lost interest. My husband would give him odd jobs to do about the house and then go round with him afterwards showing him all the things he'd missed out or not done right. You know, when I came home after learning about this in the group I couldn't think of a single time either of us had taken real trouble to compliment him on the things he had achieved.'*

Even when we 'let' our children do more for themselves, we can be mercilessly swift with correction and criticism . . .

*'I now realize that every time I watched her washing herself in the bath, I'd be discouraging her. "No you haven't done that side, you can't reach." Telling her all the things she couldn't do instead of letting her learn how to do them for herself in her own time.'*

Being encouraging of children's efforts, and remembering to state what we do want rather than what we don't, is much more likely to get a positive result. Sometimes saying what we don't want acts like an unconscious instruction to do the very thing we think we're warning them against. We call out, 'Don't spill the milk!' or 'Don't fall' instead of 'Be careful with the milk' or 'Take care, it's a long way up.' and wonder why, moments later, there's a crash as milk bottles or child falls to the ground. Language has powerful effects on the unconscious: when we say 'Don't run into the road' we are asking our children to think about running into the road rather than staying on the pavement, and thinking about running into the road may be just a short step from actually doing it. Similarly with other simple statements:

• 'Don't leave that mess on the floor'

Try instead:
• 'Clear up your toys before you go out'.
• 'Be careful, you'll fall!'
Try instead:
• 'Be careful, hold on tight!'
• Don't go into each others' rooms and make a noise'
Try instead:
• 'Remember our agreement, when the babysitter comes you'll stay in your rooms and do something quietly'

It can be helpful to look at behaviour in terms of what we want. We all tend to know what we don't want but have greater difficulty in defining what we'd like . . .

*'I was not happy with the way my daughter left the bathroom — towels on the floor, ring round the bath, caps off everything. I couldn't think of anything about the state of the place that I could be positive about. Then she proudly showed me her history exercise book. It was immaculately neat. My response was instant, "That looks lovely, you certainly know how to keep your work a delight to look at and read. I wonder if you could think of the bathroom as an exercise book?" She got the point. That evening the bathroom looked (almost) civilized and she now does make a real effort to clear up after her.'*

When we stop using labels, and start describing what we see or hear instead, we start making distinctions between who our children *are* and what they are *doing*. We move from the general interpretation, 'You're being uncooperative', to the specific observation, 'Playing with your toys makes it hard when I'm trying to dress you.' Hurling labels doesn't communicate exactly what it is that's bothering us nearly as effectively as straightforward descriptions. Statements like 'Don't be so untidy' also assume that the child knows exactly what we mean by being tidy: 'I want you to pick your clothes up off the floor' is a much clearer message and gives them something concrete to act on.

Avoiding labels heightens the chance of getting positive responses from children and adults alike. No one likes being labelled — it's too like being judged and often unjust anyway.

*'My son was loafing around watching television and I accused him of being illiterate. He was obviously very hurt and he told me that in his school's general knowledge quiz he'd come second so he couldn't be illiterate. That brought me up short. I listened to him, and acknowledged his hurt feelings, and then I apologized and explained what I'd actually meant which*

## Labels

Think of a negative label you were called as a child and come up with a specific description of what you were doing to be called that.

Remember as you do this that your parents didn't know about the possible damaging effects of labels and were doing the best they could. They no more deserve blame for their behaviour than you do for *your* behaviour as a parent.

Now think of a negative label that you use with your child, and come up with a specific description of the actual behaviour that you don't like, for example, 'I don't like it when you shout at me and call me names,' rather than 'Don't be so rude!'

*was that I was disappointed he never reads novels or literature,* *just books about cars or things to do with his schoolwork.'*

'I was labelled as the clever, studious one in the family and consequently spent a lot of time worrying about schoolwork, exams, etc., and working extremely hard. I have always found it very difficult to cope with failure of any sort.'

In our experience, children will resist even 'good' labels. 'One time', Pat Slade remembers, 'I fixed something and my mother said "Ah, you're the Fixer", and I resented it terribly. I didn't want to be the Fixer. I knew I'd have to be it the next time and the time after that. I didn't want the role or the job. It would have been nice if she could have just said, "That was very helpful. Thank you." '

To make up for the fact that they are so quick to criticize their children and so slow to encourage them, some parents go overboard on praise

'I felt as a child that I had very little praise from either parent. So that was the one thing I was going to be determined to do: when I had kids, I'd praise them!' says Ros. 'I was always careful not to put my daughter down, but I also thought if I praised her enough — told her she was brilliant and beautiful — that's what I'd get back.'

So she'd praise her daughter whenever she could, 'I thought the bigger the adjective, the better she'd feel, but it didn't work out that way. It turned out I was just encouraging Susan to have such high expectations — "What a beautiful picture", "You got a certificate in gymnastics, that's BRILLIANT". It's escalated to the point where she's now really nervous to make any mistakes. It seems to have set up a tension inside her that she's always got to be wonderful to deserve this praise — otherwise it might dry up.

'It got to the point where Susan's teacher came to me and said could I investigate ways I could help her become more independent. Well a more independent child you couldn't hope to meet. At home. But it seems that when she's at school, she's constantly asking "Am I doing it right? Is this how you do it?" If she doesn't get praise she wonders what she's done wrong.

'Now when Susan has done well at school, I say, "I bet you're pleased", letting her know those are her own triumphs, or "I'm glad you're enjoying that subject." '

'Good' labels can be as burden-some as 'bad' ones: it can be as difficult to live up to the label of being a 'bright' child as down to being a 'naughty' one. When parents continually praise their children, reserving their warm approving words for something 'good' that that child has said or done, a powerful conditional *if* gets written onto the child's self-esteem. '*If* I do this' reasons the child, 'then I'll be acceptable and loved.' Although our own research tells us that parents love their children for who they are rather than what they do, many children believe that their parent's love is attendant on them winning their approval.

Every child's wish to please is immensely strong. If they don't please simply for being themselves they will make every effort to please some other way, and so win their parents' approval. Sandra, Maureen's little girl, would always do a painting for her mother. 'What colour would *you* like, Mum?' Now Maureen tries to say, 'What colour would you like? It's your picture', encouraging Sandra to do things for her own pleasure and satisfaction, rather than for the praise she hopes to get.

Children who grow up dependent on praise live their lives doing what they think others want, never knowing what they want for themselves. Praise becomes the reward they need to motivate them to do anything. In the huge effort to please, they lose their instinctive knowledge about whether they have done something worthwhile and well. They rely on others to tell them. Their self-esteem has to be propped up because the solid foundation, 'I feel good about me' is no longer there; it has become 'I only feel good about me when you tell me I'm OK.'

*'I was very dependent on praise and approval and other people's opinions. I've always had a struggle doing things when the sole reason was because I valued them. It didn't seem enough.'*

Now with her own daughters, this mother is careful to voice what she calls 'unattached' appreciations —

warm words that are not connected to something 'good' or 'clever' that her children may have done. This lets them know they are loved and precious all the time. When they do do something well, instead of praising as she used to do, she *describes* her children's accomplishments instead.

- 'I really like the way you help me wash up, it cuts the time in half and it's so much more pleasant.'
- 'Wow, that was an amazing somersault, you landed perfectly on your feet and kept your balance.'
- 'You did that lettering a lot better, you must have worked hard on it.'

---

## The meaning of labels

Here is a list of labels. What does each mean to you in terms of behaviour — what you can see, hear and feel. For example: naughty = kicking, crying and screaming when I want her to go to bed.

- Naughty _____
- Funny _____
- Childish _____
- Demanding _____
- Good _____
- Clumsy _____
- Polite _____

*(continued overleaf)*

- Rude _____
- Dirty _____
- Lazy _____
- Bright _____
- Pernickety _____
- Bad _____
- Stubborn _____
- Neat _____
- Stupid _____
- Cheeky _____
- Grown-up _____
- Inconsiderate _____
- Bossy _____
- Rude _____
- Dominant _____
- Co-operative _____
- A tomboy _____

Don't forget to look at the labels you give yourself in terms of your own behaviour. Consider:

- Impatient _____
- Unmotivated _____
- Tolerant _____
- Competent _____
- Liberal _____
- Strict _____

*(continued top right)*

It can be very freeing to discover you are not really lazy, just wanting to stretch out and watch a film on television. Any embargo on blameful language should start with yourself. It's just as important not to label yourself and put yourself down, as not to put other people down.

## 'When I was five they gave us silver stars in school. When I was six they gave us gold ones. When I was seven I discovered you could buy stars in stationery shops.'

If we're honest, we may also find that we don't just use good labels when we want to express our heartfelt pleasure in our children's achievements. As with 'bad' labels, we sometimes use praise manipulatively, as much as a bribe to repeat that 'good behaviour' as a reward for being 'good' in the first place. We use sweets or sweet words as reinforcements to get our children to behave more as we'd like. Behavioural psychologists know all about it. They do it with rats!

## What's the intention?

The next time you have the urge to praise, stop yourself and ask what's going on? What is your intention? Do you really want to say something for its own sake? Or do you want to persuade your children to repeat what they were doing, or to change their behaviour, to suit you?

When we first introduce the possible down-side of praise, parents quite naturally protest. 'I see why I shouldn't tell my child she's stupid', they say, 'but why do I have to give up telling her she's terrific or clever?'

Labels, whether put-down or praise say 'You are . . .' They make an evaluation. They reflect an inequality in the relationship — between adults just as often as between adults and children.

*My mother-in-law is always praising me — I look nice, the house looks nice, the dinner was lovely — and I find it really*

## Instead of labels. . .

Read each situation carefully, visualizing it, hearing what might have been said and getting a feel for it and then voice your appreciation, describing in detail what you see, hear or feel.

Example: you arrive home to discover your eight-year-old has taken an important telephone message for you.
*Parent* (instead of 'Good boy!'): 'That was a long and complicated message you took from Mrs Jones. You wrote it so clearly that I knew what I had to do to be prepared for the meeting. I really appreciated it, thank you.'

- Your child has been having trouble coping with some aspects of his schoolwork. Recently you have noticed an improvement in the marks.

  _____

  _____

- You've been to see your child perform in a school concert/play. Afterwards he comes running and asks, 'Was I good?'

  _____

  _____

- On a wet half-term day, your child has spent a long time drawing and making things, giving you some time to get on with what you want to do.

  _____

  _____

- Your child remembered your birthday, bought you a small gift and wrapped it up himself.

  _____

  _____

*irritating and patronizing. It's like she's standing in judgement over me, grading me according to how well I do.'*

As with blaming labels, we find it can be helpful to avoid praising labels by being more specific; describing our children's triumphs and successes and letting them know how we feel about it.

It also helps if we are clear in our own minds whether we're expressing spontaneous appreciation of the child, ('You're so funny and great, I love you!') or of something he's done, ('I like the way you used those bright colours together in your drawing'). If we tend to save our praise for 'praiseworthy' bits of behaviour, it's no wonder children draw the conclusion that we only feel warmly towards them when they act in a certain way.

It's difficult to begin with. Parents come to us and say, 'You know, this thing about labelling — I can't get away from it! I don't know what to say to my son when he comes home with these pictures that he's done at school. I say "That's lovely" and I could bite my tongue off. And I say to myself, "There I go again, labelling." '

Adele Faber and Elaine Mazlish, who have described making the transition from evaluative praise to descriptive praise, show that if we keep praise words out of our vocabulary, the child's own good

feelings about what he's done start to come forward.

'My four-year-old came home from nursery school, shoved a page of pencilled scribble under my nose and asked "Is it good?" My first reaction was an automatic "Very good." Then I remembered, "No, I've got to describe." I wondered "How do you describe scribble?" I said, "Well, I see you went circle, circle, circle, wiggle, wiggle, wiggle, dot, dot, dot, dot, dot, dot, slash, slash." "Yeah", he nodded enthusiastically. I said, "How did you ever think to do that?" He thought for a while and said, "Because I'm an artist!" '

Labels are so much a part of the climate children are brought up in these days, it's impossible to avoid them entirely — either on our own part or those around us. Nevertheless, every little helps. If children are encouraged to value themselves and their achievements in their own right, they will then have enough self-esteem to deal with put-downs by rejecting them instead of taking them on board.

*'When I lose my temper and tell my son he is silly. He tells me, "I am not silly." Then I wake up and apologize, realize there is a lot of difference between the fact that he sometimes does silly things and he is silly.'*

It is all too easy to get caught in the trap of blaming ourselves for using labels — labelling ourselves as useless! It inevitably takes time to change the old ways. We should aim to be as lenient on ourselves as we now hope to be towards our children.

## 'Becoming aware of all the different ways you could say things, I found it helpful and alarming.'

Words are only one way of getting across positive and negative messages. *How* we say them can have just as much impact — if not more. In our society, a great deal of emphasis is placed on *words* and much less on the attitudes and emotions underlying them — though these will leak out whether we want them to or not.

Studies have shown repeatedly that words are often the *least* important part of what's being said. The way our face looks or tone of voice changes carries much more impact. These unspoken elements of our communication betray our innermost thoughts, feelings and motivations in a way that can make them apparent to everyone *but* ourselves.

Unspoken messages are very powerful. Dr Ray Birdwhistel, the American anthropologist who coined the phrase 'body language', analysed a series of interactions on a one-to-one level and in groups to try and establish what percentage of the communication was verbal — relayed by the words — and what was non-verbal. He divided what was being 'said' into words, or content, tone of voice, facial and body expression, movement of hands, arms and legs.

His conclusions were that the words accounted for just 7 per cent of the total impact! Tone of voice accounted for 23 per cent and facial and body expression for 35 per cent each. Although these ratios are obviously approximate, and he himself has acknowledged as much, they do reveal just how much else we communicate over and on top of the words we use.

Children communicate how they are feeling in unspoken ways just as much as adults do.

*'When my son gets angry, he very quietly destroys something. Once he took a pair of scissors and cut a big hole in the front of my nightie. Later, he told me, "I didn't want you to die but I did want you to be very cold indeed."'*

We communicate attitudes — what we are *really* thinking or feeling —

## What you say and what you mean

Think of as many different ways as you can of saying the following sentences without changing the words. Many can be said in such a way as to reverse the meaning completely:

- 'Yes, dear, of course you can go'
- 'I hate you'
- 'Oh be quiet and go and get into bed'
- 'If you do that again you will be in for real trouble!'

with our faces and bodies as much as our words. When we sit back and look straight at the other person without interrupting, turning away or fidgeting, we signal 'I'm attentive, I'm interested in what you have to say, I'm going to take notice of you.' These instinctive things we do to put other adults at their ease are considered plain good manners. Yet, how often do we extend a similar courtesy to our children? When they come to us wanting to talk or to share a problem how often do we put all our attention on what they have to say? Or do we just continue with the washing up or whatever we happen to be doing without even turning round to look?

*There are times when I think I'm willing to give them attention. But, in fact, often, often, I'm not really available. There are so many times when they say, "Look, Mum, look!" and I look for a moment, and because they don't get on with it immediately, whether it's a double skip or standing on one leg or something, I start chopping the carrots again. Then they say, "You're not looking, look, Mum, look!" So why can't I just say, "Sod the carrots" and give them my whole-hearted attention?'*

Children, start off at an automatic disadvantage – being so much smaller than us. In the groups, we often play a simple game (which we have included here for you to try out yourself) in which two adults talk with one another for a while, one standing and the other kneeling. Some find it a revelation. 'It was a very strange feeling, talking to another grown-up who was towering above me.' Most agree that they feel more comfortable standing up. 'It seems more difficult to be taken seriously when you are being looked down upon;

hard to convince somebody right up there that you are serious about something.' For one woman, that feeling of being the child also connected with how she felt 'about a lot of men who are very big, tall and macho, I feel like a little girl, I just fall into that role.' Another found that the one who was standing up asked all the questions while the one who was sitting or kneeling felt compelled to answer, 'rather like an interview'.

---

## Game (to be played in pairs)

Find a partner, another adult or one of your own children. One of you kneel and other stand. If you are doing this with one of your children, place him on a stool or a chair and you kneel down so the difference in height between you is reversed.

Now hold a conversation! It can be about anything you like but continue it for three to five minutes. Time it, and then change over.

Afterwards talk about how you felt.

---

For everyone in the groups, this game illustrates the simple influence a difference in height can have on the way we get on together. 'It was a very good reminder that it is important to get down to their level, physically, once in a while', said one mother who went home and tried it out with her son, first with a big height difference between them and then on the same level. She reported that the second way was 'immediately different — less of a confrontation with me being the stronger one, dominating the space, and more friendly because more equal.'

By getting down to his level, becoming more like him, this mother was unconsciously 'mirroring' or 'reflecting' her son. People who have made a study of the ways we communicate have found that when people get on well together they tend to 'mirror' the way the other person is sitting or standing or talking. We can observe this for ourselves by watching people who are closely engaged in conversation. Notice how alike their stances and gestures are, how they will tend to lean forward or back, cross legs or arms, pick up glasses or teacups, in such a synchronized way that it almost seems as if their movements have been choreographed for them. It's thought that this unconscious copying creates a sympathetic symmetry that puts the other at his ease. It reassures him that he is acknowledged and accepted, communicates not just 'You're OK' but 'I share some of how you're feeling and I'm prepared to move some way towards being like you.'

We can make use of this observation with our children. Being prepared to get down to a child's level, lowering our voice when they are being quiet or even getting involved in what they are doing as we talk with them are all ways of communicating our acceptance of them, our willingness to listen to what they have to say. Although getting down to a child's level, or bringing him up to ours if he is small, is an obvious place to start, we can also mirror our children in other ways. Here are some examples that have come up in the groups.

*'It had never occurred to me that maybe my four-year-old just can't keep up with the flow of words when I am explaining things to him, so I've slowed down to talk to him at a rate much more like that he uses himself. It makes all the difference when I want him to take in what I'm saying.'*

*'I've found that it made a lot of difference to be able to slow down and do things at toddler pace when we spend time together. Instead of pulling him along as I have become conscious of doing when I'm in a hurry, I now let him pull me along. In the process, I've found that I notice so much more of what is going on around us. It's a different world! By rushing around all the time I missed out on all the tiny creatures and plants that he was witnessing in his casual journey through life.'*

*'My son winges and whines at the end of the day. I really can't stand it. I know that he wants to be listened to or cuddled or is tired but it irritates me. Well, the other day, instead of letting it get to me I knelt down on the floor and started doing it with him. We started grunting together and got it up to a crescendo. And it was funny, so we did it two or three times more, and it completely changed everything.'*

## Summary

- Poor communication is one of the main dissatisfactions of family life.

- Often we are acutely aware of what's going wrong in our communication with others but are unable to change it because we have nothing to put in its place.

- Communication 'skills' offer alternatives.

- Some people are naturally more skillful at communicating than others. We can help ourselves by borrowing some of their skills and making them our own.

- Conflicts in our relationships can be intensified by the belief that we should always be consistent in our responses to our children.

- This can lead us to say 'No' when we mean (or feel) 'Yes' and 'Yes' when we mean (or feel) 'No' and to start imposing all sorts of rules and restrictions we don't at heart agree with. Children find this more confusing than the straightforward inconsistency of all human behaviour.

- We therefore believe that consistency of *attitude* is more useful than consistency of *reaction* and that if we aim for honesty in our dealings with our children they will pick up the underlying consistency.

- All of us get into the patterns of acting and reacting, parents particularly. Sometimes these are useful, even life-saving; other times, they cause us to behave in ways we later regret.

- We can help ourselves break out of unuseful patterns, and substitute new ways of behaving, by taking a deep breath and then letting it out; this gives us time to consider responding in some other way.

- One of the most unuseful habits parents tend to get into, without even knowing it, is to label their children.

- These labels can become prophetic: if we tell our children often enough that they are stupid, clumsy, uncoordinated or slow learners they will find it hard not to fall in with our expectations.

- Even 'good' labels do our children a disservice and may encourage them to grow up dependent on praise, rather than secure in the knowledge that whoever they are, and whatever they undertake, is worthwhile for its own sake.

- To avoid 'bad' (critical) labels and 'good' (praising) labels it is helpful to concentrate on describing the behaviour — what we see, hear and feel — instead.

- There are other ways of communicating besides words and these often have more power. They include tone of voice, posture, gestures and facial expression.

- Children are particularly good at picking up the unspoken elements of our communication especially when these are at variance with what we are actually saying. If we want to avoid sending mixed messages we need to be confident that the spoken and unspoken parts of our messages agree.

- We can make use of this by adapting our unspoken elements of communication. Getting down on a level with our children when we are talking to them, for example, shows them that we have time for them and are interested in what they have to say.

# CHAPTER 4

# LISTENING, AND HELPING OUR CHILDREN

'As a society, we still believe children should be seen and not heard. We don't allow children to talk and express their views.'

As a group, children and young people have very little voice in this world. Whether at home or at school, there are frighteningly few people willing and available to listen to what they feel or want; frighteningly few children who grow up confident that they will get a fair hearing.

The recent focus on child abuse, and the way these cases are heard in court, underlines how little attention we pay to a child's testimony. 'It is disgraceful that the law is so heavily weighted against the evidence of a child', said a father in September 1987 when his son, though willing to testify against a man who had assaulted him, wasn't called forward, while the man went on to be acquitted. 'How can you explain to your son that the law which grown-ups have

made says a child's evidence isn't as good as a grown-up's?'

It is rare enough that adults listen to each other, but it almost never happens that adults really pay attention to what a child is telling them; much less take the trouble to enquire about their opinions and points of view.

*My son actually says, "But, Mummy, you're not listening!" and now I realize why. I'm getting dressed, putting my shoes and socks on or whatever, and Tom comes in and I don't really want to listen to him at that time of the morning because I'm too busy thinking of what I have to do, then my husband comes in and just talks over my son's head, because he's rushing out and needs to tell me something,* and all the while I'm saying to my son, "Yes, of course I'm listening." '

Just thinking back to our own childhoods will remind us how frustrating and demoralizing it was not to have our point of view taken into account.

*'It had never really occurred to me to find out what my children thought or felt about "family" decisions or our life together. My husband and I took all the decisions, considering them too small and inexperienced to make any serious contribution to ideas or discussions. It was our job to give them what we thought was the best possible upbringing. Until I thought about it during the parent group it had never occurred to me that it should be any other way.'*

As a skill, listening is probably the single most important item in our parent support groups. Certainly, just becoming aware of the real value of listening and from there really attending one hundred per cent often has the most impact on the quality of family life.

*'I had always thought of myself as a "good listener", never realizing how many times I was shutting up the other person just by the way I was listening. I became very aware of how frequently I interrupt and impose my ideas on people. I also realized what a poor listener my mother was — and why I'd never been able to talk to her about my problems.'*

Many parents consider themselves good listeners and genuinely believe they spend a lot of time listening to their children. Yet, when they start to become aware, they actually discover *they* are the ones doing most of the talking — telling their children how they feel rather than waiting to be told, rushing in unasked with reassurances and words of comfort, contradicting when they don't like what they hear...

When they start really making an effort to attend wholeheartedly to what their children are telling them, many parents say they find it much more difficult than they ever expected.

'I know full well when someone's listening to me and when they've just switched off, there's such a dramatic difference', said one mother, who had a big insight the day she realized that she never really made herself available to listen to her children when they came home from school. 'I used to *think* I was there for them but I was sitting on the phone all the time. And there was always chaos and fighting and unpleasantness. Now I actually take the phone off the hook and we sit round the table

together while they have something to eat and I give them my full attention.'

Listening *is* hard. It goes right against everything we learn: at school we are taught to be ready with our answer in case the teacher asks us a question; at home we learn to compete for speaking time with other members of the family; as adults, we spend a great deal of our listening time rehearsing what we are going to say next, waiting for the very next chance to jump in with our own point of view. No wonder conversations between adults so often seem to run on two entirely separate tracks, with neither listening to the other, both talking at once — butting in, interrupting, 'Oh, that happened to you? Well, you should have seen what happened to me ...' Summing it up perfectly, the writer Nathan Miller has declared that conversation has become a competitive exercise 'in which the first person to draw a breath is declared the listener'.

Research surveys confirm that people rarely take in much of what is being said, even when it is of some importance to them. In one experiment, patients in a doctor's surgery were questioned just five minutes after their consultation had ended. They were able to remember only half of what the doctor had said to them. When what people hear is of less personal consequence to them, they probably absorb even less.

There are good reasons for this. The mind races well ahead of the speed of speech, processing words about four times as fast as the mouth can say them. This means that however fast the other person talks, there's always plenty of free time for thinking. Even when we are eager to listen to what others have to say, keeping the mind at talking pace is a real challenge. Before we know it, we're caught up with our own thoughts and have lost track of what the other is saying. Our eyes glaze over and off we drift. The problem is often made worse because we don't know how to avoid having to listen when we don't want to; we don't know how to say 'No' without offending. At such moments, pretending to listen is the easiest answer.

---

## To listen or not?

Can you identify what you do when you are not interested in listening to what is being said, when you do it and who with? How often do you pretend to be attentive and interested because you don't know how not to without offending?

As you become more aware of when and why you want to stop listening and do something else, you might like to consider how you could tell the other person in a way that won't offend them.

---

Gradually, as our awareness increases we will begin to be able to take much more positive decisions about when we want to listen and when we don't.

*I'm much clearer about when I'm listening and when I'm not. Looking back, I used to spend an awful lot of time in that half-and-half state.'*

Listening is rare and being listened to a luxury. Although learning how to listen is one of the most valuable gifts we can give our children, it often goes right against the grain simply to let them talk uninterrupted. As parents, we want so much to help, teach, advise and reassure that it goes against all our instincts to keep quiet and let our children do the talking. We have what communications consultant, Robert Bolton, calls 'interfer-iority complexes'.

*'My idea of being a perfect mother is to sort out all difficulties and iron out any distress. I've always found it so uncomfortable to think of Sandra having any pain or unhappi-*

## Being listened to

As you think about how attentive a listener you are, you might find it useful to recall what it is like to be listened to — both attentively and otherwise. Most of us at some time in our lives have had at least one experience of talking to someone about something important to us and feeling really listened to and helped. We will have also had many experiences of trying to get a message across to someone who just wasn't there for us, not concerned with what we were telling them at all. You might like to take a moment to think about what was different about those moments of good attention — how the other person responded and how you felt as a result.

*ness. If she tries to tell me she's feeling shy or sad or lonely or left out, I feel dreadful too. Everything in me rushes to take that pain and that problem away, so she can feel better.'*

When children have a problem of some kind, many parents feel that it's part of their role as a parent to come up with solutions that will make them feel better. 'I am so consumed with anxiety that things won't go well for them', confessed another mother, 'that's my Achilles heel as a parent, I'm so terribly concerned for my kids all the time.'

As a result, parents often persist in providing what they think their children want, or need, regardless of strong messages that they would actually like the opposite. Mary Amersham and her husband had their daughter Ann's IQ tested when she was very little, and it was so high that they felt they had an obligation to pay for her to go to the best school in the area, so they scraped and saved and sent her to the most academic school in the neighbourhood. At no stage, however, did they think of discussing schools with her or listen to what she wanted.

Mary told the group that when Ann was just three and in nursery school she actually told her parents she didn't like the reading class, she preferred sticking and gluing. 'But we didn't listen', said Mary, 'and when the head teacher wanted her to jump a year, the second year of infants, which was practically only sticking and gluing, we agreed very readily.

'And do you know? She's been

trying to tell us ever since that she enjoys arts and crafts and doing things with her hands, but we didn't listen because she was bright and so she couldn't possibly be artistic as well. As far as we were concerned, these two things were mutually exclusive.'

It was only after Mary joined our parent support group that she actually *heard* what her daughter was telling her for the first time. 'Ann was saying "I know I'm a scholarship girl, which saves on half the fees, but I don't want to carry on at this school, I'd rather go somewhere else where I can do pottery and needlework and cookery." Up to that point, I didn't even know that she wanted more emphasis on art. I wanted so much for her to have everything I never had, I had set my heart on her going to university. Now, over the last year or so, Ann has gradually dropped into my ear, "I don't really want to go to university, I'd rather go to art school." Two years ago I wouldn't have considered it. Art school was for academic drop-outs.'

Many parents are deaf to what their children tell them. They discount what their children say, making light of their fears and anxieties, not accepting the way they feel.

*'I remember having nightmares as a child, and having my fear brushed aside and being told off because I was disturbing the others by crying. When my son, Mike, has a nightmare and says there is a ghost upstairs in the attic, there is a ghost, for him — I can't dismiss that. I can't calm him down and make him feel better by telling him there's nothing there.'*

Many parents are dismissive of what their children try to tell them because it challenges their own concepts and values and makes them feel uncomfortable.

*'I used to lecture Andrew about what he should be feeling rather than accepting what he was feeling. When the perennial problem of going to school came up, I would wheel out the old arguments about how useful school is, and what he should be doing there, rather than letting him talk about why he doesn't want to go and the fears and feelings he has.'*

In the short term, it is easy to feel, like this father, that it's part of the parental role to educate our offspring in how they should be feeling. By expecting them to think and feel like little versions of ourselves we maintain the safety of our own lives. Children who are fully independent in the way they feel and think threaten our values and ideas. It means we are no longer in control, when being in control is so often expected of us. In the long term, however, discouraging our children from feeling and thinking for themselves goes right against our goal of wanting them to grow into fully independent adults.

Children, like adults, want to be listened to, to have their feelings and thoughts accepted and acknowledged. Though they may eventually give up if their overtures are repeatedly rebuffed, they will be irrespressible in their efforts to communicate. 'Sandra grabs my face! I have to listen!' said one mother, painfully aware now of how often she unthinkingly dismisses or contradicts what her daughter is telling her.

'When Sandra comes in from school at lunchtime, saying "Nobody likes me at nursery, Mum", my impulse is to say immediately, "Of course they like you, you're a lovely girl, of course they want to play with you." But when I reassure her with what I think, or perhaps hope, is the truth, she gets even more upset. "No! Nobody likes me at all. They all think I'm horrid." '

To begin with, some parents worry that acknowledging feelings of loneliness or being left out, without 'correcting' them, will reinforce their children's fears and insecurities. Infact, allowing these painful and difficult feelings to be expressed (painful and difficult though it sometimes is) is to accept our children in a way that ultimately builds up their self-esteem rather than belittles it.

## 'So few parents have the feeling that children are capable people. You know, we just think of them as children, and the concept of children equals inability to deal with life.'

All parents want their children to grow up resourceful and self-reliant, confident of their own judgement and abilities. Yet the way they respond often unintentionally conveys the opposite. When we criticize, advise or reassure, and particularly when we tell our children what to do, we tell them as clearly as if we had said it out loud that we do not believe they are capable of tackling their problems on their own.

## Unspoken messages

Unspoken messages are very powerful. When your child comes home from school sobbing, you could respond in hundreds of different ways. Here are five, each likely to be met with very different reactions. See if you can match these spoken messages with the unspoken ones below the line:

- 'Got into trouble at school again today?'
- 'You poor thing. Tell you what, I'll make you a nice jam sandwich and then we'll watch TV together . . .'
- 'Something seems to be upsetting you. Do you want to tell me about it?'
- 'Tears won't solve anything. Let's look at this objectively.'
- 'Come on. Cheer up. Everything will be all right tomorrow.'

---

- 'I've had much more experience at this sort of thing than you, so listen to me and you'll get to learn how to deal with it.'
- 'I know exactly what your problem is. I can see right through you!'
- 'I don't like to see you so unhappy, put on a smile for Mummy so that at least one of us feels better.'
- 'I can see you are unhappy. If you would like to talk about it, I'm here to listen. If you don't want to talk, I can respect that too.'
- 'Whatever it is that's upsetting you is unimportant. You're making a fuss about nothing.'

When we start to gain an awareness of the things we say to our children, we realize that they often go right against the sort of things we want them to grow up thinking and believing about themselves. We call these unhelpful messages 'risk responses'. Unfortunately, they are *very* common. Indeed, they sum up all that is most characteristic of many adults' communication with children, particularly children with problems. they can be divided into three groups:

# Judging/blaming/criticizing

Labelling, fault-finding and criticizing, ('You should have apologized' 'Why didn't you hand the project in on time, dumbo?') put the child down, reinforcing feelings of hopelessness and failure. When children are already feeling bad they don't need to be made to feel worse. There are times when 'constructive criticism' can be constructive, but they are much fewer than many adults think.

# Playing the expert

Diagnosing and playing the amateur psychiatrist ('Got into trouble at school again today?'), ordering, threatening, moralizing and giving information unasked, all communicate our belief in our own superiority as a solver of problems. 'You just shut up and let me sort this one out for you' is the unspoken message and even further beyond that, 'You're not capable of sorting out your problems and living your own life.' Firing questions communicates the attitude, 'Just let me get enough information and I'll come up with the answer for you.' However helpful, however (at times) screamingly obvious our own solutions, they won't be nearly as effective as the solutions our children pick for themselves.

# Diverting and reassuring

Dismissive reactions ('Come on, there's nothing to worry about'), and changes of subject, ('Let's go and see what's for tea') push the child's problem and feelings aside as though they were of no consequence. Reassuring appears to give comfort but often it simply drives the problem beneath the surface — we feel better, they don't.

Risk responses are not 'good' or 'bad' in themselves. Sometimes — usually when there isn't a problem, they may be entirely appropriate. There are times when we will need to find out what is going on and to question; times when our children need information and it would be unfair to withhold it, though this type of information is usually asked for; times when using logic can teach enormously. There are times, too, when sharing a joke that labels or name-calls is the very essence of family togetherness.

It's when there is a problem and our children are upset or troubled, that these responses risk adding to their hurt and upset feelings. Sadly, communications experts estimate that when people go to others with their problems they are met with these responses about 90 per cent of the time. They are certainly familiar to the parents in our groups judging from the groans of recognition. Every parent tends to have their 'favourite'. When these are explored, they often turn out to be attitudes picked up from their own parents — even if they remember hating being treated like that and vowing never to do the same.

Faced with the unusefulness of these responses it is all too easy to feel guilty for having used them and for still using them. Parents in the groups need to be reminded that they have been doing the best they know how, and even as we learn to do something different, no blame needs to be attached to the past.

So how can we respond in a helpful, risk-free way? One of the biggest surprises is that often we can help *most* by saying *least*. 'I always thought that people expected a response when they were telling me about their problems. I felt I had to come out with something', said one of the women in the groups, adding that she also felt resentful that the person she was 'helping' would never do what she suggested anyway. Then she started listening full-time, staying silent except for the odd 'mm' or 'I see', and to her surprise not one of her friends accused her

of being uninterested. They even thanked her for helping!

Jamie Russell's father took him to the school sportsday. Jamie was running in one of the races. He was a very fast runner, one of the school's best, and was hot favourite to win, but he tripped and stumbled and ended coming almost last. He was bitterly disappointed and felt miserable. His father, hating to see his son so upset, tried to cheer him up. 'Don't worry, you did your best. You ran really well.' And Jamie felt worse and worse. He later said that he didn't *want* his father to make him feel better. He knew he'd made a mess of it. He just wanted him to understand how miserable he felt.

It's not just children who need to have their feelings acknowledged. When this example came up in the group, one woman said she knew just how Jamie felt. Instead of listening to how she was feeling whenever she'd had a bad day with her three young children, her husband would try and jolly her along. 'He'd reassure me, say "But you're a marvellous mother", and that wasn't the point. So I'd start getting resentful towards him — the one person I'd been looking forward to seeing all day — and he'd react by getting cross too, saying "Well, it's not my fault. What can I do about it? I can't do anything you know", and I'd be screaming at him with rage and frustration, "I don't want you to *do* anything. I just want you to acknowledge the fact that I've had a rotten day." '

Naturally, her husband couldn't understand what had got into her. He felt upset in his own turn. After all, he'd only been trying to help. Parents also find it difficult when those things they do with the express intention of helping their children have the opposite effect; when the things they say to encourage them to 'open up' shut them up instead; when the most innocently-meant question sparks off a 'Huh! You never listen!' and the child stomps off.

The truth is that saying something, is nearly always riskier than saying nothing; remaining silent can have a powerful helping effect.

*'My thirteen-year-old daughter came home from school very upset. She threw her satchel on the floor, stomped through the hall and out of the back door. I followed her out and found her sitting on the back steps, looking hurt and upset and very close to tears. I had to resist trying to help in the old ways and sat down beside her to see if she wanted to talk. I wanted her to know I was there and loved her and would help if she needed me. After ten minutes, she sighed a huge sigh, stood up, stretched, smiled and said. "Thanks for listening, Mum." and went inside.'*

---

## Giving full attention

At times when in the past you would have perhaps started questioning your child about why she was upset, try just inviting her to talk. Sit down somewhere and let her know you are ready and wanting to listen. Put aside whatever you are doing and concentrate completely, face to face, on what she is telling you. Let her talk. Listen silently, giving her your full attention. Notice what her body posture is telling you and her face. Listen to the tone of her voice as well as what she says.

How did it feel just to listen? Did you have to bite your tongue? If so, what did you want to say and for whose benefit? The most common 'want' is to ask questions. Ask yourself why you felt you needed to ask questions; how could they have helped?

# 'Don't just say something, stand there!'
## (Haim Ginot)

Helping our children when they have a problem often means saying, and doing, less rather than more. It was summed up by one parent as 'not so much helping as not stopping' - an active *enabling* that lets the child move on through the area of hurt and distress towards a solution of their own choosing.

Children, young children especially, aren't always as fluent and forthcoming as we'd like. They are hesitant, contradictory, often silent. Many grown-ups feel uncomfortable with silence. The minute there's a lull, up pops the interfer-iority complex and in they rush with words and questions. They want to *say something* to show that they care, that they *are* listening. Until they try staying silent, parents worry that it will discourage their children, that they'll interpret their lack of words as lack of interest.

*'I found the power of silence, just shutting up, absolutely amazing! I've been a chatterbox all my life, but now I'm learning the value of being silent. I used to leap in with questions and advice all the time, especially with Ann. I set myself up as the world's most helpful and perfect mother. As soon as I saw a solution to a problem, I'd interrupt whatever Ann was saying so I could tell her what to do.'*

This mother discovered that words weren't the only way of showing that she cared. She could invite Ann's confidence simply by *showing* that she had time for her — stopping whatever she was doing, and giving her full attention; communicating her readiness to listen by nodding her head, saying 'I see' and 'mm'; nudging her forward when she seemed stuck with 'And . . .?' 'Oh?' or 'Go on' or even repeating key words from her daughter's last sentence to encourage her to continue, such as 'I don't know what's happening. I just feel stuck.', 'Stuck?'

She found that questions could be useful too — not the inter-rogation-type risk responses she had been using, but 'open' questions such as 'Would it help to talk about it?' Open questions are those that leave the conversation wide open so that the child can decide what, and how much, she wants to share with us. They invite her to expand upon whatever is on her mind, giving the message 'Anything you want to talk about, that's fine with me.'

If we say 'What's the matter *now*?' or start firing leading questions, 'Got into trouble again at school today?' we risk a defensive reaction. We also risk taking the conversation off-course in the direction of our choosing rather than towards the problem that's concerning her. Because these 'closed' questions are often used to confirm something that we are already thinking, 'Had a bad fight with the boyfriend, darling?' they can also make assumptions and carry blame: 'What did you do to make your sister cry?'

---

## Open and closed questions

Here are three pairs of questions. See if you can identify which is open and which is closed

* 'That looks like it hurts — does it?'                    ☐Open ☐Closed
  'What have you gone and ridden your bike
  into *now*?'                                             ☐Open ☐Closed
* 'You seem upset. What's up?'                             ☐Open ☐Closed
  'Have you been arguing with your sister?'                ☐Open ☐Closed
* 'Those equations getting the better of
  you again?'                                              ☐Open ☐Closed
  'What is it about your homework you
  find hard?'                                              ☐Open ☐Closed

---

'I used to say "Why?" all the time. It's the most deadening question. Now I'm more likely to say "What was it about the day you didn't like?" or just "You seem upset",' said one mother, who tried out the new way with her son Roger one evening. 'He was very agitated, doing the washing up with tremendous concentration and intensity. I just leaned against the sink and said "Want to talk about it?" He carried on with the washing up, so I stayed there. I didn't know what else to do, but I didn't go away. And there was a long silence and Roger went on washing up. And then he started talking about what was bothering him, and I just grunted and "mmed" a bit and he stopped a while and then he came back to the subject and talked some more about it.'

Because open questions are non-directive, they leave plenty of space for children to explore what's on their minds, without being driven into one corner or another, and to tell us, *if they choose*. There's no cast-iron way of guaranteeing their confidence, however. Invitations to talk won't always be accepted, however beautifully they are phrased!

*'I used to fire questions at Andrew as soon as he came in from school, "Did you do this? How was that? Who did you play with?" and he'd respond by getting more and more withdrawn and sullen. Now I am learning not to go in full-tilt with questions. I just say something like, "Do you want to tell me about today?" and sometimes he does and sometimes he says "NO"! And I have to accept that he doesn't feel like giving me any information about his school-day. If I've given him an open-ended question, I have to shut up when I get a negative reply . . ."*

## 'I feel really sick about what happened. It's upset you a lot . . .'

One of the most useful skills we introduce to the groups is known as reflective listening. This is the verbal equivalent of mirroring how people sit or stand. It entails 'reflecting' back, briefly and concisely, the essence of what the other person is expressing. Many people use it quite unconsciously. When we're taking down a telephone number or directions to a friend's house, for example, we'll repeat what we've just heard to check we've got the details right. We can also use reflective listening to let our children know that we've heard what they are saying and that their thoughts and feelings are accepted. This can be a big step forward for parents who regularly argue with, or contradict, what their children are saying.

*'My daughter is always complaining she's tired. I used to say "You're not tired. Let's go outside and play", and she'd just go on and on whinging. Now when she does it, I get down to her level and say, "You're tired. You're really worn out. It's been a long day", and that stops her. It's as though she feels that I've heard what she's saying so she doesn't need to keep on telling me.'*

When we introduce the idea of reflecting back what their children are saying, some parents are incredulous. 'Are you serious?' they ask. 'My children will think I'm mad if I just repeat what they've said.' We ask them to try it out and let us know how their children react.

*'I finally plucked up courage to try the reflective listening with Dick when he was complaining about his sister. Not only did he not notice I was doing anything strange, but we actually spent five minutes together, him just talking and me listening, snuggled up on the settee — for probably the first time in weeks. I am quite sure he was better tempered that afternoon than in a long while.'*

We advise parents that the most effective reflections tend to be those that put what their child has just said in a different way. It's straight repetition that sounds automatic and parrot-like. It also helps to be brief — one sentence, if possible. Short responses are less likely to take the conversation off track. Here's an example from one mother:

*Dot:* 'I don't want to go to school any more.'
*Mother*: 'You don't ever want to go again."
*Dot:* 'No I don't like it.'
*Mother*: 'You didn't enjoy it today?'
*Dot:* 'I was the only one who didn't help paint the green dragon.'
*Mother*: 'Everyone else had a go and you didn't.'
*Dot*: 'Yes, but I don't think Mrs Clarke saw me. I think I'll tell her tomorrow. (Silence.) I do like it really 'cos we're going to name the goldfish tomorrow.'

To begin with, reflective listening is bound to feel awkward. One consolation is that it nearly always sounds a lot stranger to our own ears than it does to the person we are listening to — they're usually just thankful to have what they say accepted for once. To get over the problem of repeating what their children have just told them, many parents find it helps to have lead-ins, phrases that provide an opening for a reflective statement. Examples might be:

* 'Sounds as though you're feeling . . .'
* 'I imagine you're . . .'
* 'It seems to me like you are . . .'
* 'What I hear you saying is . . .'

Having a formula to start off with has been compared to having scaffolding on a house — necessary to begin with for the support it provides but quite able to be removed once your own responses are sufficiently strong to stand on their own and you settle into the style that suits you best. Here's another example:

Joe is seven and gets teased a lot because of a nervous twitch he has developed in the last few months. He comes storming in from a game in the park: (the dialogue has been cut)
*Joe:* (angrily) 'I hate Mark.'

*Mum*: 'Sounds like you're upset with him.'

*Joe:* 'He's so nasty to me — I don't do anything to him and he just picks on me.'

*Mum*: 'That must feel pretty miserable.'

*Joe*: 'It's so unfair, he knows I can't stop it, but he just uses it to get at me.' (close to tears)

*Mum*: 'I can see that's pretty painful for you.'

*Joe*: 'I just wish I could get rid of it.'

*Mum*: 'Its pretty frustrating not being able to control it.'

*Joe*: 'Can you help me find a way to stop?'

*Mum*: 'I'll certainly help you try and find a way.'

Because reflective listening formalizes the listening role and the talking role, many parents find that it helps make clearer the boundary between themselves and their children. It made a real change in family life for one mother of six boys especially her relationship with the eldest, Nicky.

'He's always getting furious, stomping off, shouting rude things, slamming the doors, throwing the laundry basket downstairs. Normally I get furious, too, and start shouting, and the volume just goes up and up. Now I find it easier, not easy but easier, to detach myself and switch off. I say to myself, "It's his problem" and ask myself how he's feeling rather than tuning into my own feelings of irritation and frustration. The laundry always seems to get picked up anyway.'

There's often another, unlooked for, benefit: when we start listening, really listening, to what our children tell us, we find out more about them and what makes them tick, what's important in their lives, who their friends are, what they care about. The result is often a friendlier, more equal, relationship. It seems that once we put ourselves beside our children, rather than opposite them in the usual interrogation mode, we often find ourselves more in tune with them, more like equals than adversaries.

*'My daughter came into the kitchen, saying something about she hadn't been chosen for dancing. Last week or the week before I might have just said, "Oh, I'm sorry about that" and got on with whatever I was doing. This time I said, "Oh that must be a disappointment", and she said "Yes, it is." And you know, she carried on, saying how it was she hadn't been chosen and who had been chosen and how she felt.'*

# 'What if I don't get it right?'

When people start reflective listening they often worry that they are not doing it properly. It can be a blessing to find that they don't have to get it right. They can misinterpret things, be totally off target and still be less likely to divert, distract or shut their children up than if they were to leap in with questions or criticism.

Firing questions risks steering the other person away from what is really bothering her. An inappropriate reflective response does the opposite. It brings her right back to *how she's feeling now* and encourages her to clarify it so that we can understand her better. As long as we keep whatever we say brief and to the point, she will just correct the misinterpretation and continue.

*'Diana was supposed to be going round to a friend's house but seemed really reluctant so I sat down with her at the kitchen table to explore what was going wrong — at one point the conversation went something like this:*

Diana: *"I'm fed up with going to Helen's."*
Me: *"You've gone off Helen then?"*
Diana: *"No of course I haven't gone off her. It's getting there that's the problem."*

*The fact that I'd got it wrong didn't matter — she just brought us back to the real subject, which was about some boys she had to pass along the way.'*

Once they become comfortable with the approach, many parents find it a huge relief to let go of the directing role. All they have to do is *listen*. Even so, it can sometimes take a while to realize that it's not up to them to decide where the conversation goes or to come up with the answers.

*'I used to struggle when I was reflective listening. All the time I would be asking myself, "What on earth do I do next? What's the most appropriate response?" and by the time I'd prepared the paraphrase, the person who was talking would have gone way past the point onto something else. To begin with, I missed a lot of what my children were saying. And then I realized that I was trying to control and direct the conversation instead of remaining with it and letting them go where they wanted.'*

Being accepting of and listening to our child is not the same as condoning what she says or does. Some parents worry that reflective listening can only 'work' if they agree with what their children are saying. One mother, for example, found it hard to practise reflective listening to her three-year-old if she felt he was getting worked up over something 'trivial'. 'One of the most difficult things for me was getting into the routine of saying what appeared to be stupid things back to him', she admitted.

It took a while for her to adjust perspective. 'Then one day we were playing a little game where we were tracing letters. We were doing the word CHAIR when he started getting angry with himself because his letters weren't as good as mine; they were a bit wobbly. He started to yell. Before, I might have thought "Now he's going over the top" and told him to snap out of it or dismissed it saying, "Come on, Miles, it doesn't matter", which of course it didn't. To me. But this time I managed to bite my tongue and stopped and thought and said exactly the opposite. "It does matter to you. I know you like everything to be perfect", and he said, "Yes, I do" and began to cry, but he didn't start chucking everything across the room like he usually does or start scribbling on the rest of the game. It really seemed to help.'

Reflective listening is one of the safest and most effective ways of allowing children to express hurt and angry feelings, but first we have to acknowledge that those feelings, exist, however violent or hurtful to us; to say 'I can see you're very angry about that' or 'You really hate me.'

This, of course, runs counter to the prevailing attitude that 'bad' and 'negative' feelings are best dealt with by pretending they don't exist — denying them, forgetting them, 'rising above' them. Whereas adults tend to be very inhibited about showing their feelings, young children express their raw emotions very readily. For them, acting and reacting are one and the same. Soon, however, they learn that it's not OK to be angry or to cry. Although they don't stop experiencing these emotions, they will start to deal with them differently — instead of getting them out of their system, they may push them down below the surface. Some call this 'learning to be civilized.'

*'It was a revelation to me how much of the time I try to prevent my children expressing what I consider to be negative feelings. When they are upset or angry, my natural reaction is to comfort them and calm them down, to say "Look, everything's going to be all right." It was hard just to let the hurt and upset feelings be, to allow them to have feelings that I'd prefer them not to have.'*

Now when this mother's children have tantrums and get cross and upset, she lets them cry and tries to see it from their point of view. 'I reflective listen, not in words necessarily but moaning with them or crying with them, at a very simple noise level almost. And, you know, I've discovered it's quite fun to lie down on the floor and kick your arms and legs around and let go!'

*'Learning to be angry, and how to get it over with, is one of the most valuable gifts my children have taught me. I never learned it from my own parents. There I learned that anger was something that you kept right inside yourself. If you were my Mother you sulked for about five days, and if your were my Dad you were quite frightening when you were angry so that didn't do either. To see a child get absolutely furious, get it all out and then get over it, was a great relief for me. I discovered I could do that. I could have a temper tantrum!'*

It's very difficult to let our children express their feelings if we're very guarded about expressing our own. Many adults find it hard to live with feelings they consider 'not nice', unreasonable, even shameful; to accept that these feelings have a right to exist. We believe feelings cannot be labelled 'right' or 'wrong'. They just are. What's important is how we express — or repress — them. The biggest breakthrough in the programme for one woman was in allowing herself to have feelings she previously spent most of her time denying.

*'My mother-in-law is an absolute bitch. I've always felt so bad and guilty for hating her. Then I let my husband know how I was feeling and he just said, "Oh, OK, fine." Now I'm allowed to loathe my mother-in-law even though she's a poor ill old lady, I'm finding that my relationship with her is actually better. I feel I can even arrange to have her to stay with us in the near future as long as I don't have to go on with the pretence of getting on with her.'*

Although this woman feels it was

her husband accepting how she felt that made all the difference, nobody gave her permission to have, or not to have, these 'bad' feelings *except herself*. The interesting thing is that now she can accept how she feels, without making big judgements about it, she can be more accepting of the way her children feel as well.

'All the time I was fighting my own feelings, I couldn't allow my

---

## Feelings

As a child were you given permission to feel? What sort of response did you get when you were feeling:

• Angry and violent

_____

• Happy and excited

_____

• Confident and full of yourself

_____

• Quiet and withdrawn

_____

• Curious and into everything

_____

• Bored

_____

• Sad and lonely

_____

• Scared

_____

• Hurt and ill

_____

• Soft and loving

_____

• Loud and boisterous?

_____

children to feel anything that was mean or nasty. I would feel angry and get at them, telling them they didn't feel like that about their friends or each other. They had to be nice people *all the time*.'

Emotion has been called 'energy-in-motion'. When we accept and express that energy, we allow it to move on and the experience to pass. When we deny it, we push it down beneath the surface where it stays festering, often building up beyond all proportion and finally exploding in a violent outburst that we may later regret.

Children's feelings, unlike adults', are amazingly short-lived, especially young children's. When we let children express their feelings without telling them to pull themselves together or to snap out of it, we tell them it's OK to have those feelings and give them a safe space to let them go.

Three-year-old Richard Stevens came running in from the garden yelling that he had hurt his foot. 'Instead of comforting him, I started reflecting his feelings', said his father. 'He was angry more than upset or hurt, angry that it had happened. The world was against him. So I said, "You're really cross . . ." and it seemed to take the pain away. He got up and ran back out to play.'

Some parents fear that reflecting back their children's feelings will aggravate the hurt by opening up old wounds. They worry that drawing attention to upset feelings will needlessly prolong their children's unhappiness and get in the way of them becoming their old sunny selves again. In fact, reflecting back feelings is a very powerful, and rapid, way of allowing children to let go of them.

Many parents also shy away from the thought of their children suffering and want to spare them every unhappiness, not realizing that suffering can be a valuable learning and growing experience — helping them to deal with a painful side of life and teaching empathy towards the sufferings of others.

Children don't even have to be able to talk to be able to understand when their feelings are being accepted and acknowledged. Lily Graham's daughter, Sheila, had tantrums from the age of about one, terrible screaming fits. The paediatrician she took her to told her that the only way to deal with them was to leave her in her room on her own until she stopped, but Lily resisted. 'I felt that this would be cutting myself off from her just when she needed me most and yet I felt so helpless, completely swamped. I couldn't see what else to do. I knew she was feeling furious and unhappy and frustrated but I couldn't understand why, couldn't do anything to help.

'One day, Sheila had a tantrum, was down on the floor screaming and yelling and thrashing around, so I got down on the floor and thrashed around with her and said, "You're really angry, aren't you? You hate Mummy, don't you?" and she just stared at me and gradually got quieter and quieter and stopped. I couldn't believe it. It just released all the tension. It was like she knew that she had got her point across.'

Being accepting of our children means accepting how they are feeling, whatever they are feeling, but it doesn't mean having to approve of how they choose to *express* those feelings. It's not giving them *carte blanche* to beat someone up whenever they feel bad! This is an important distinction for parents who find many of their children's ways of expressing anger and frustration completely unacceptable.

*'I was worried that reflecting Miles' emotions would stir them up and make them worse — encouraging him to lash out at me or at other children when-ever he felt bad. Now when he gets angry and frustrated and goes over the top, we let him know that it's OK for him to feel bad and angry. But it's not OK to hit me, or anyone else, when he feels like that. We say, "No, you don't hit me when you are angry but it's fine for you to be angry".'*

When we reflective listen to feelings, we may not always have a spoken lead. We have to judge from the unspoken messages and clues our children are sending us.

*'When Peter broke his arm I had to stay overnight in hospital and couldn't pre-warn Dot. The following day when Dot came home from school she was untypically hitting me and punching me and generally throwing things around. I said "You're really angry with me for not being here last night aren't you?" Immediately the anger subsided, she burst into tears, flung her arms around me and said "I missed you."'*

'When my kids were little, I soon learnt that there was very little point trying to get them organized when they were having a tantrum. I could say "Pull yourself together" until I was blue in the face. There was no way that they *could* pull themselves together.'

Using reflective listening for hurt and angry feelings sometimes acts as a prelude to solving the problem itself. When any of us, adults as well as children, gets upset, we often need to express the emotion before we can turn our minds to solving the problem. We get so emotionally 'flooded', that we can't think straight.

A normal calm state of mind has some balance between the emotional and rational sides. When we become very emotional, the rational part of the mind gets squeezed out and we can't think straight.

One of the women in the groups found this out for herself when she was seventeen and walking home from school. 'A man jumped out in the road and tried to strangle me. I struggled and got away and knocked on a stranger's door. I asked her if I could use the phone. When she said "Yes", I realized I couldn't remember my phone number. I was too upset to function on that level at all.'

She kept that incident in mind when her son Roger ran back home from school after being harassed by a small group of older boys. 'He came in very upset indeed. When I saw him I felt so angry, I wanted to smack the faces of those boys for worrying my little boy', but instead of letting her feelings dictate the situation or bombarding Roger with questions like 'Who are these boys?' or 'Exactly what happened?', she reflective listened when handling his upset feelings. 'He was

flooded with emotions. I knew it would be useless to try and reach the rational side of him which was just drowning at that point, so I used reflective listening to help him come out with his feelings and calm down.'

'When he was calmer, we thought of all the possible solutions there could be. We both put in ideas and wrote them down. Then Roger went through the list and threw out the ones that wouldn't work, saying, "That won't work, I can't do that, it will only make things worse" and then he finally said, "That *might* work" against the suggestion that he and his friends get together and sort it out. But he was adamant that I shouldn't go to the school and see the teachers and try to sort it out for him.'

It's not just children who need to have their feelings listened to before they can be in a situation to understand and take in information. One doctor who joined our parent support group told us that he had often been on ward rounds where the consultant would stop by a new patient's bed for a chat and ask, 'Have you any questions?' and the patient would say 'Yes' and ask something and the junior doctor would interject, 'But I told them that when they were admitted last night', not realizing that the patient may have been told it but he didn't *hear* it: he was too emotionally overloaded to take it in.

# 'The more you can listen, the more likely you are to find the *real* problem.'

Sometimes, often, the problem a child seems to have won't be what's really worrying her. Problems are like onions, with layer upon layer concealing the real problem at the heart of it. People who are really upset or worried rarely talk about their deepest worries straight off; instead, they test the water, sounding things out before they risk revealing themselves more fully. This is why, in the 'helping' professions — nursing, social work, psychotherapy — people are trained to look beneath what is called the 'presenting' problem.

Children are no different. Peter Clough used to come home from school really tense some days. 'I used to get kicked and punched or Dot would get blamed for everything', explained his mother, then she used reflective listening with him and was amazed by the outcome.

*Mother:* 'You're feeling really angry inside'
*Peter:* 'I hate you and Dot's being really horrible to me.'
*Mother:* 'You feel Dot's being nasty to you.'
*Peter:* 'Yes, she's really annoying me.'
*Mother:* 'What is it she's doing that you find annoying?'

*Peter:* 'I don't know, just go away.'
*Mother:* 'You want me to leave you alone?'
*Peter (crying a lot):* 'No.'
*Mother:* 'Is there something else?'
*Peter:* 'Yes, I hate school.'
*Mother:* 'You really don't like it.'
*Peter:* 'No, it's horrid.'
*Mother:* 'Anything in particular?'
*Peter:* 'Yes, playtime.'
*Mother:* 'You don't like playing outside with the other children.'
*Peter:* 'It's not that, it's Mrs H. the dinner lady.'
*Mother:* 'I thought you really liked her.'
*Peter:* 'No, I hate her.'
*Mother:* 'You don't like her any more.'
*Peter:* 'No. She told me off today because they wanted to clear the playground for a lorry to drive in and I ran the wrong way and she really shouted at me.'
*Mother:* You felt hurt and embarrassed.'
*Peter:* 'Yes.'

Reflective listening helps move people through these early indirect stages to the real problem, the heart of the onion.

*'My son told me he didn't want me to go on all these parents'*

weekends. I thought it was because he didn't like not having
me there at home with him. He'd
complained about me going off
before, but perhaps because I
felt a bit guilty about it or
perhaps because I had a commitment to finish the course, I was
slow to listen to him.

'When I did, what a revelation!
It turned out he wasn't at all
upset about me not being home!
He was worried about missing
his Friday evening swimming lesson. He's working towards his
fifty-metre badge because his
father has said that once he's got
it, he will take him sailing. I
would never have learned that if
I'd launched in with reassurances
and justifications. Once I knew
what the real problem was, I suggested he went with a friend of
his, and his mum, but he only
wanted to go with Jim or me. So
then we looked at the calendar
to see which weekends I would
be away, and we found he would
only be missing one lesson
because it turned out that the
only two other Fridays fell in the
school holidays when there
weren't swimming lessons anyway.'

Because the problems children
come up with are so often not
what's really troubling them, it's
especially important to try and
stop ourselves jumping in pre-
maturely with reassurances or
advice.

'I went to pick up my youngest
child, Juliet, from a friend's and
I could tell she was determined
from the second she saw me that
she was going to have a tantrum.
We got in the car, and she started to whimper and I said, "I can
tell you feel awful, I know it's just
dreadful for you at the moment,
all you want to do is scream."
And she cried harder and then
she said, "Yes, and you didn't
collect me from school." It was
the first time I hadn't collected
her from school myself. I had
asked a friend whether she
could pick her up and I would
collect her from there. That was
what the whole thing was about
and the moment it came out, it
was finished. I explained, "I'm
sorry', I had a doctor's appoint-
ment and I couldn't be there, and
that was the best I could do" and
we agreed together that next
time I would let her know in the
morning if someone else was
going to be picking her up.'

Even if we can listen to the problems as they arise and get to the
heart of the onion as it were, finding a solution isn't always possible.
Lots of parents find it very hard to
say, 'Seems as if we can't sort this
out right now, we're going to have
to wait a while for the answer to
come up.'

*'The other day, a magician was coming to Sandra's school and she was finding it very scary — something to do with magicians not liking children and putting them in cages or making them vanish; ideas that I'm sure she's got from watching cartoons on the television. I told her that magicians like working with children, which is why they choose to go to parties and schools. I listened to her fears and gave her information about what magicians do and are like that she didn't have. I didn't reassure her or try to take away her anxiety — she was still scared — all I could do was reflect it back and say "Yes you are scared." Then the morning the magician was due to come, she made up a song about it. She was sitting in the back of the car singing it and she said "I'm not frightened any more. I made up a song about it."'*

Problem solving is a process, often an ongoing one that may take more than one session to complete.

*'Sometimes I start listening to Andrew and I come up against, "I don't know." Often he doesn't seem to know. It's only by going through the process that he finds out. Sometimes the answers surface slowly over time, weeks and weeks of occasional listening.'*

'I felt very self-conscious using reflective listening with Peter, but once I got on to the moving-forward questions we were away and it worked fantastically. He would frequently get to the "I don't know" or "go away" stage and I found I could move him forward from this and continue reflective listening.'

Sometimes straight reflection is not enough. We can get to the point where we get stuck. 'So you're feeling upset?' 'Yes, I'm feeling upset', 'You're feeling really fed up and bad inside?' and the child starts to look at us as though we are either mad or hard of hearing. There comes a point where we need to break out of the circle and nudge the child on again. So that when we say 'So you don't want to go to school?' and our child confirms 'No I don't want to go to school' we can move on, as Peter's mum did on page 125, with an open question like 'What is it about going to school that you don't like?' This still lets Peter work through his problem, without mum's interference, but helps him move on from one step to the next.

When the people we are listening to come up with statements that have a hopeless air of finality — 'But I couldn't do that', 'Oh, well *that's* impossible' — we can supplement our reflective listening with a gentle challenge in a way that doesn't contradict or correct them, but brings them up short and encourages them to rethink some of their assumptions.

- 'I have to stay here.'
  'Who says that you have to stay here?'

- 'Nobody loves me.'
  'You think nobody loves you - how do you know?'

- 'I couldn't do that.'
  'What stops you?'

Here is an example from one parent:

*Martin:* 'I hate maths lessons!'
*Dad:* 'Your maths giving you a problem?'
*Martin:* 'Yeah. I never seem to be able to get things right.'
*Dad:* 'I expect you feel pretty useless at maths.'
*Martin:* 'Sometimes Mr Graham just expects too much and I can't keep up.'
*Dad:* 'You'd like him to give you more time.'
*Martin:* 'I know he won't, he expects us all to work fast.'
*Dad:* 'I hear you say he won't give you more time — and I wonder how you know that for sure?'
*Martin:* 'Well I don't know for sure, but I can't ask him.'
*Dad:* 'You don't think it would be right to ask him. I wonder what would happen if you did?'
*Martin (after a pause):* 'Well, nothing really I suppose. Maybe I'll try before the next lesson.'

Again and again, parents' experiences with reflective listening show that their children will come up with their own answers to their own problems, once they're given the chance. They don't have to act as much more than a sounding board.

*'Jane said, "I don't want to go to the playground. The others won't let me join their club. First they say I can and then they say I can't and they change their minds." I hurt for her, but I just said, "That must be very confusing for you when they can't make up their minds whether they want you in with them or not." And Jane just said, "Yes, it is. I know what I'm going to do. I'm going to start my own club!"'*

Even when we are called upon to help, we can let our children have the benefit of our knowledge and experience without taking over completely. We can say 'Now I wonder what's the best thing to do Can you think of anything?' and give them *time* to have some ideas themselves before contributing our own. If we don't leap in too quickly with our solutions, we may find that our children do come up with their own.

*'We were at a friend's house for the afternoon recently and Diana asked if she could stay the night. I said that was fine but that I wouldn't be staying. Several times in the next hour she came up to me and said, "Mummy please let me stay." Once or twice, I repeated that she could of course stay if she wanted to and then I realized what must be going on for her and I said, "You're feeling uncertain about whether you want to stay or not." She replied, "Part of me wants to stay here and part of me wants to come home with you." I said, "Yes, that must be very difficult for you and it's your decision and I shall be going home in about half an hour. You can make up your mind in that time." She decided to come home and stay another time.'*

At other times, when children seem really stuck we can reinforce our intention of not sorting everything out for them: 'It's your problem. I can't tell you what to do about it, that's up to you, but how about if I suggest some of the things that maybe I'd do if it was my problem?' Even when they are very little — two, three, four — and cannot think of anything much themselves, this still introduces them to the idea that they *could*. 'I'll think of some things and you see if you can think of some things.'

Four-year-old Jane Slade had been having recurring nightmares about snakes and would wake up in the middle of the night absolutely terrified.

*Mother:* 'That must be very frightening for you, you don't like them do you?'
*Jane (sobbing):* 'No, they're horrible.'
*Mother:* 'What would you like to do to them?'
*Jane (thinking for a while):* 'I'd like to bash them on the head!'
*Mother:* 'How would you do that?'
*Jane:* 'I'd bash them on the head with a hammer!'

Jane's mother found a hammer and at Jane's suggestion put it under Jane's pillow where it stayed until the nightmares stopped and Jane felt she didn't need it any more.

'I find it very difficult not to try and get answers.
Reflective listening has shown me how often I look for
a solution rather than allowing my children to express
fully what they feel, and hearing them out.'

Sometimes there won't be an immediate solution to the problems our children have. This may in itself be part of the process. They may need to mull over the problem before discovering something new and useful for themselves or they may need lots more talking time before they begin to find their way out of whatever it is that is troubling them. 'They might still feel down or fed up', said one mother of her listening sessions, 'but that's life. A nice clean result is not always possible.' Even so, it can be hard for modern achievement-oriented parents to be satisfied with an inconclusive session. They want a 'result'.

The problem with becoming focussed on the possible end-point is that we miss what's happening on the way. One parent who tended to fix upon the end-result, actually had to forego reflective listening with her son's biggest problem because she could only foresee one solution and that was unacceptable to her.

*John doesn't like going to school. I know why. He's got certain fears. But whenever I try and reflective listen, we never get beyond "I don't like going to school." I've discovered that it's not appropriate to reflective listen him when I really don't want to know what's up. It seems useless to probe. He has to go to school.'*

Another mother in the group also had a child who didn't like to go to school but she dealt with it rather differently.

*'One day we were just standing outside the classroom door and I said, "You seem to be upset about going to school. It can be hard sometimes." I just acknowledged that it's hard to have to do something you don't want to and he said "Yeah, but there's nothing you can do about it, is there Mum?" and ran off.'*

Reflective listening can be very revealing — not just in the sense of what our children share with us, but what it tells us about our own feelings and motives. Several people in the groups have found that their efforts at reflective listening have given some unexpected insights. One mother, for example, found that she would 'listen' to her children in order to get her own way, to direct them towards the solution *she* wanted.

*'I knew what I wanted from them from the start. It felt like I was humouring them. I thought, let them have their say, then we'll do what I want.'*

Nearly all parents soon discover that listening to their children in this new way, though often rewarding, is not always comfortable. It hurts to hear their children's distress, without changing the subject or jollying them out of it. Now that they sometimes have to listen to what they would rather not hear, they can no longer insulate themselves from what makes them feel hurt.

*'I would listen to Grant for such long periods of time, I came to know intimately what the problem was: he felt deserted at the breakup of my marriage to his mother. Seeing him in such a desperate state made me feel so sad – and guilty. His pain was so great and yet there was no practical way to help him. There were many moments when I wished I could have just turned a blind eye like the old days and cajoled him along, pretending it would be all better, or at least persuaded him that it wasn't as bad as he made out.'*

Reflective listening takes time and practice — and a preparedness to feel a little clumsy and self-conscious at times. To begin with, we have to stop and think and make a deliberate choice about whether or not we are going to use it. We feel our way, practising reflective listening when it seems appropriate and when we remember to; changing our style gradually, a step at a time, by being silent more, perhaps, and trying out some responses as it feels more comfortable. Every time we practise reflective listening with our children and get a positive response, it builds our confidence and makes it that much easier and more natural the next time round.

Some parents may feel they are being insincere, 'More like a professional dealing with a client than a mother with a daughter' was how one mother put it. 'It's all so cool and controlled. I'm worried that she'll feel I don't care.' When questioned, however, it turned out that the fourteen-year-old daughter of this mother had no idea that a 'skill' was being used on her. The experience of being listened to reflectively, even by a beginner like her mother, was such a relief that she was not conscious of anything being false or unnatural. She was just relieved to be able to say how she felt. 'She was just less, well, motherish', she added, when asked.

At other times, children are only too aware that we are trying something new, especially if they're older and used to us acting and reacting in certain set ways. In this context, even the mildest change of style can feel quite threatening. They may be resistant or sceptical, greeting attempts to help with remarks like 'Don't use that stuff on me!' In such cases, it can sometimes help to let them know how important it is for us to find a new way of communicating with them, and ask for their co-operation while we do it.

It can also help to temper our enthusiasm and to practise reflective listening only when we feel it's really needed, when there really is a problem they need help with. Overdoing it to make up for lost time, as some parents do, can soon prompt remarks like 'There she is, off again!' or 'Why don't you ever talk to me properly any more?'

At other times, when conversations may fail to develop, we need to consider the possibility that it's not our children who have a need to talk, but us who have a need to be confided in. When we get the following scenario — 'I don't want to talk', 'You don't want to tell me what's wrong?', 'No' — it's time to recognize that their need for privacy may be stronger than their need to be listened to. In the true spirit of democracy and accep-tance we can't force our children to respond!

Sometimes, anyway, it won't be appropriate to reflective listen. When we feel so angry or upset or threatened by what we hear that we have a problem too, we will need to deal with our own feelings *before* we can detach ourselves sufficiently to listen to theirs. At these moments, a useful little trick is to practise reflective listen-ing ourselves. Our listening part can work away for a moment or two in a dialogue inside our head with the upset part, with sur-prisingly useful results.

*'When I become aware of a feel-ing that's uncomfortable, fear or worry or distress, I make a pic-ture of myself looking worried or fearful or whatever. Often it's a young me, and I talk to it and I say "You're feeling frightened" and the me says "Sure am" and we talk. Sometimes I cuddle it.'*

*'Sometimes I get so drawn into a situation that I forget that actually it's only one part of me that is feeling that way, and that outside that situation, there are lots of different parts of me that can cope and help if I can bring them in.'*

Practising reflective listening on ourselves is quite different from the stiff unsympathetic 'talking-tos' most of us give ourselves when we are upset or anxious. It's much more supportive for a start. Mostly our internal dialogue runs in a much more critical and unaccepting mode, such as 'You're so stupid', or we simply shut off the bad feelings, as though by refusing to acknowledge them they will somehow miraculously go away.

*'I listen to myself much more than I used to and I notice much more how I'm feeling. I think, "Ah, interesting, I need to cry about that." I've found it a profoundly helpful process because I'm so much more aware of what's going on inside me than I used to be.'*

It may also be good to let our children know that at the moment we are feeling very upset, having trouble dealing with what is going on inside us and have to let it out or let it subside before we can help them.

Reflective listening takes time. If we are preoccupied, rather than listening half-heartedly, one ear open, mind on something else, it is much better to be quite honest about how we feel (there are some ideas to help with this in the next chapter.) We can let our children know that we would *like* to listen but have something else on our mind or have to get something done, and suggest a time when we might get together to talk.

## Summary

- Listening is considered the least important of all our social skills, so it's hardly surprising that most of us are not very accomplished at it.

- Becoming a parent can intensify some of the difficulties we have in listening to what is being said to us.

- This is because it is very hard to remain detached and let our children say all they want without butting in to advise or reassure them.

- Though silence is especially uncomfortable for exactly this reason, most of the time it's less of a risk than words.

- Another helpful way of responding is to reflect back what our children are saying in our own words. This lets them know we have heard what they say and accept how they feel.

- Getting our response 'wrong' usually doesn't matter at all. In fact, it's a lot less risky than questioning, diagnosing, reassuring and so on because our children can simply correct us and continue.

- Reflecting feelings, even if our children aren't expressing them in words, is especially helpful. Strong feelings stop children thinking straight and get in the way of their being able to solve their problems. Reflective listening can defuse these feelings and so act as a first step to solving the problem.

- This means allowing children to express feelings that we may judge to be trivial, over-exaggerated, nasty, negative or destructive.

- Often when we use reflective listening to deal with a problem, what first appeared to be the problem will simply be the first layer. The real problem may be way underneath. We can get there sometimes by reflective listening in stages, sometimes over several days.

- Reflective listening tells us a lot about ourselves, our motives and our assumptions about our role as a parent.

- It also makes us vulnerable. If we dare to listen in a true spirit of openness, we risk having our values, attitudes and beliefs questioned and, perhaps, permanently changed. We also risk feeling the hurt and pain our children feel.

- We are bound to feel self-conscious to begin with, but the people we listen to are much more likely to feel conscious of being helped and be grateful for it than be aware of having been the subject of a new technique.

- Reflective listening is only appropriate if we are feeling loving and accepting. If we are feeling rushed, fed up, resentful towards the other person, then we shouldn't try it.

# CHAPTER 5

# SPEAKING OUR MINDS AND HELPING OURSELVES

'I always thought you had to be totally giving all the time. It's a relief to know that you don't have to be, because it's such an impossible goal. I know I can't be a non-stop attentive mother. If I don't give myself some time, I just get ratty and resentful and no one's happy.'

People who join our parent support groups rarely give much thought to their own needs. They come because they want to learn how to be even better parents and to do even more for their children. Although they do not come for themselves, that's often where their need is greatest and where the relationship stands to gain most.

*'My relationship with my children is getting better not by focusing on them and what I can do for them but focusing on me and what I can do for me. I'd always been aware that children need a very good example, but I wasn't so aware that the example had to be me going off and doing things for myself and getting what I want out of life.'*

Another mother's experience was even more marked: 'I had decided it wasn't OK for me to sit and read a book if Johnny wanted my attention', said June Hargreaves, 'I had to play what games he wanted to play, watch what he wanted on television, listen to what he wanted on the record player and, of course, he got to have very high expectations of me as entertainer. And I'd be sitting there feeling really bullied. I've never been bullied like that in my life. My brother was nothing compared to John.'

Afraid of causing conflicts that would spoil their close relationship, June let John's behaviour go completely unchecked. She became exhausted and resentful. John got more and more out of hand. Then June joined our parent support group and the day they looked at the whole question of needs — the child's needs and the parent's needs and at how the parent's needs are also important — a door opened for her. June remembered how her mother had totally submerged her own needs to bring up her children and how burdened she had felt by the knowledge of what her mother had given up for them: 'I felt totally in her debt. She was so giving all the time, there wasn't room for anyone else to be generous.'

When June finally gave herself permission to do the things *she* wanted to do — nothing extreme or very selfish, just going out occasionally in the evenings, getting a babysitter in and taking up some home-based part-time work — she not only felt immediately better but her relationship with John improved as well.

'Now when I don't want to play with him, when I'm not prepared to give him my full attention, I'll say so. I'll say "I'm doing this now, so I'm not going to play", and it feels marvellous not to feel so totally dominated by him. He seems to have found it a relief as well. It can't have been happy for him to be bullying me either. Now he can be another way, too.'

Of course, it didn't all change overnight. There are still times when the relationship gets a little lop-sided, but because June is more aware of what is happening, she takes action and it soon rights itself again.

'The other evening, I wanted to go to a party that was quite important to me but I'd been out the night before and felt it was a bit much for John, so I stayed at home wishing and wishing I'd gone and by the time I put him to bed, I was feeling so fed up and so resentful, that we ended up having a row with me shouting and saying unpleasant things.

'Now I realize that when I go out and get what I want, I'm much better company and much nicer to him. Really pleased to see him again. It's as though my batteries have been recharged and I've got something to give. If I'm not getting enough, our whole relationship is filled with resentment.'

There are many parents like June — people who have somehow stopped looking after themselves and counting their own needs as important.

*'My sister is totally submerged by her husband and four children. Whenever I ring her and ask how she is, she goes into*

*a long description about how
each of the children are. She'll
go on for an hour if I let her. Even
when I interrupt and repeat my
question, "No, I didn't ask how
they are, how are you?" she
doesn't really tell me how she
is.'*

Many parents feel guilty about
doing things for themselves
because they have persuaded
themselves that a parent's role
should be a totally giving one. They
don't question what the consequences are for their children of
having parents who are constantly
forcing themselves to go without.

'I've given too much to
parenthood, ignored my own
needs', said one mother reflectively who has a nearly grown-up
daughter and two stepsons. 'It has
built up resentment and soured my
relationships.' Through the group,
she has become aware that only
once she's given herself some time

and attention can her attention be
fully with her daughter. 'If I listen
to myself I can listen to her. If I
have needs that aren't being met, I
find it very difficult to be a patient,
listening mother.'

Unfortunately, when parents
start looking after themselves they
are bucking a strong cultural trend.
There are powerful unwritten
rules in our society that state that
'good' mothers put their children
first, *all the time*, regardless of
whether this order of priorities is
actually in the best interests of
the children.

'I knew that I was just helping to
perpetuate the problem of macho
selfish men by giving in to everything my sons demanded,' said one
woman, 'but I haven't known how
to change it without being
unnecessarily brutal.' It can be
doubly hard for mothers like this to
shift the status quo because they
get so little practice at asserting
what they need.

## 'Hey, I'm a person too!'

Assertiveness training is now an
accepted idea for people wanting
to get ahead in business — women
especially — offering them the confidence to go for what they want
and furnishing ways of handling
others, both below and above them
on the career ladder, that are both
productive and tactful.

It's not just at work, however,
that these qualities are in short
supply. Many parents find it hard
to assert what they want in a firm,
gentle way with their children and,
as a result, either go overboard —
screaming and shouting and laying
down the law — or wearily submit
to having their own needs walked

over, yet again. As a result, they find themselves feeling just as under-valued and bullied as any cor-porate underdog and just as much at a loss for how to change things, without becoming bullying and dominating themselves.

*'When I was a child I was always on the receiving end. I thought, "Just wait till I'm in charge!", but I don't ever seem to have got to be in charge. I've learned that I can feel just as much on the receiving end as a parent.'*

This mother, like lots of parents, would benefit enormously from the assertivness skills now being taught as commonplace in com-panies. Although at first it seems an odd idea — surely managing col-leagues is one thing, fractious three-year-olds quite another — learning assertiveness in the home can make a real difference. It gives parents the confidence to deal with difficult situations without fear of flying off the handle or giv-ing up and giving in. It enables them to say 'No' and to mean it. It helps resolve the small everyday irritations — the dirty dishes, the toys on the floor, the music up too loud — that loom larger and larger until they become really *big* issues. It can also help establish limits of behaviour, and prevent problems arising, without resorting to bribes and threats.

'We didn't want to break his will to assert ourselves', said one father who joined the parent support group with his wife because their toddler was running rings round them. 'In fact, we wanted Miles to grow up with a strong will, which he had, but it was impossible to live with. We were swinging from giv-ing in because we couldn't face the hours of tantrums that would follow when we denied him some-thing, and being utterly author-itarian, which we both hated and didn't seem to have a better effect anyway.'

These parents felt desperate. This seemingly out-of-control child, not yet four, was forcing them to abandon some of their most passionately held principles about parenthood. 'The one thing we did feel strongly about was that we didn't want to smack him — ever. Then we thought, "Well, it might just do the trick." It didn't. Instead, he started smacking us back and the other children in the playgroup, too.'

When that didn't work, they had to admit defeat. Then they joined the group and found that they were alternating between the two most common styles people have of communicating their needs — aggressiveness and submissive-ness.

Although these two extremes lie at opposite ends of the scale, they can be mixed together. We all know parents who try to be firm, but after a few attempts of saying 'No', fall back on the 'easy' option of letting their children walk all over them. That continues until something snaps and they revert to becoming authoritarian again. 'Right, that's *enough!'*

*'Jane used to say to me, "One minute you're nice and the next minute you're horrible! And I don't know what's going on." And I thought, "Oh help, what do I do now?" I was trying to be so controlled, and then I was exploding and then feeling so guilty I'd be all nice again. It must have been pretty confusing for her.'*

Though it's very common to swing between these two extremes, most of us probably gravitate towards one or the other most of the time — either dictator or doormat. Identifying your habitual style, using the guidelines given below to help you, can be one of the most helpful steps towards change.

## 'Don't worry about me. You do whatever you like.'

Submissive people, anxious to avoid conflict at all costs, always defer to what others want. These are the people who want peace at any price. Although they are often described as 'selfless' or martyrs', they are actually just as responsible for *not* getting what they want as those who seize what they want with scant regard for anybody else.

Submissive people invite others to take advantage of them. It may not be a good way of getting their needs acknowledged, but there are other pay-offs. It's a comfortable and safe position. They are never the ones sticking their necks out. 'On one level it suited me to lose', admitted one woman, 'then everything that went wrong I could blame someone else for.'

People who have previously had no trouble expressing their needs, and getting them met, may change when they become a parent. June was an outgoing, extrovert sort of person who always spoke her mind. Yet she became totally submissive once John was born, submerging her own needs in order to meet his.

People who tend towards submissiveness tend to make permissive parents — lenient to a fault and, apparently, content to let the most outrageous behaviour go unchallenged. Inwardly they may be squirming or seething; outwardly the children have the whip hand. This does children few favours. Instead of learning sensitivity, they learn to disregard the needs of others. Having found out that they can get on demand, they are liable to start ordering their parents (and others) around, insisting that all their needs be met.

*'A lot of the time, my son's behaviour is completely unacceptable. I feel very resentful towards him, like a victim, that he is controlling me and I am powerless over him ... all those things that my mother was and that I never dreamed I would become. Of course I love my son, but there is a lot of hate there as well. A lot. It's like a stone inside me.'*

Although submissiveness is un-likely to be met with outright hostility, it's no guarantee of being liked. Excessive sacrifice for others can breed resentment and so produces the very thing this type of parent doesn't want — rejection.

This was a revelation to one mother who had always believed she should give herself totally to her children, going along with whatever they wanted regardless of how she felt. It wasn't until she started to stand up for herself that she got the positive responses she had always been looking for. She realized that her children actually respected her far more when she stood up for what she wanted rather than taking everything they threw at her.

## 'Do what I want, or else.'

At the other end of the scale are the people who have no trouble fighting for what they want, and getting it. The problem is that they make their needs known, and get them met, at everyone else's expense.

One way to describe these people is 'aggressive'. We all know someone who fits the description - good at telling others what to do, who is, convinced of his own rightness and very quick to blame others when things go wrong. This person will also tend to shout a lot and lose his temper. This can be quite effective, but the price can be high: battered self-esteem and hurt feelings for those on the receiving end *and* resentment towards the person who made them feel that way.

Aggressive types make domineering parents who like to have total power and control over their children. They often believe, genuinely, that they know what is best for them and will tell them in no uncertain terms what to feel, think, believe and do. Some quite reasonable and considerate people become authoritarian as parents because of the models they had as

children. They fear that if they give an inch their children will take a mile: 'For me there is this fear that I won't be able to cope if I am more flexible', said one parent who, despite wanting to act in quite another manner, has got into the habit of using threats and punishments to get her children to do what she wants.

She is already discovering that as her children grow older, this strategy is getting less successful. The punishments and threats that were effective when her children were young and too small and too powerless to object, seem to have lost their power. Her children are now unimpressed by her threats or challenge her to carry them out, pushing her to the point when she realizes she has no more threats to use.

*'Last year I was furious when a friend told me she had seen my son go into an amusement arcade that he had been strictly forbidden to go to. I didn't know what to do. I had already taken away his bicycle, restricted his television time, cut his pocket money ... what was left? I had run out of power over him!'*

Children of parents who act aggressively towards them, react by becoming defensive — just as subordinate colleagues do when their overbearing boss flies off the handle. They may either grow up so cowed and lacking in confidence that they find it difficult to take responsibility for their lives or, become increasingly rebellious, resentful and defiant — striking back at the previously powerful

## Submissiveness v aggressiveness game

**The game:** to be played with someone you feel at ease with, a friend, a child or your partner. Think of a situation where one person is trying to get his way over another and take turns playing submissive and aggressive roles, right down to the way you stand and what you say. Keep the roles up for at least five minutes, and preferably fifteen, to give yourself a chance to get really immersed in them. Walk around, do simple things like making a cup of tea and serving the person you are with. Or demanding one if you are playing the aggressive role!

**The roles:** (these are exaggerated to make the point)
*Submissive* types are hesitant, speak so softly it's hard to hear what they are saying and creep around in an effort not be noticed. Everything they do is an apology for their existence. Submissive people say, 'I don't know, you decide', 'That's all right with me' (when it's not), 'I'm so sorry if I put you out at all . . .', 'Don't worry about me, you do what you have to do, I'm quite happy to sit at home' (and suffer!) Even when they do try — tentatively — to make their desires known, they mumble and cover their mouths and look at their feet or preface it with an apology, 'Sorry, but could you . . .?' or tail off lamely at the end of their sentences or contradict themselves, 'but you do whatever you like'.

*Aggressive* types stand up and lean forward in an attacking stance. They may shout and they use the word 'You' a lot in a blaming sort of way. They say 'Can't you do anything right?', 'Get me the book that's on the desk, will you', 'Stop that noise, you're driving me mad'.

*Afterwards*: talk about how you felt in each role. Which was the most comfortable for you? Which felt most familiar? How much did you identify with the behaviour that you, or the other person, was portraying? Children tend to be very good at this game. It can be enlightening to watch them 'pretending' to be bossy or Mummy when she gets angry.

parent by lying, covering up and forming alliances.

*'Dad had the power in our family because we were all frightened of him but as we got older we pulled against it. When I was a teenager I had many threats from him with the result that I became totally rebellious and pushed against them as hard as I could.'*

Communications experts estimate that some 95 per cent of us gravitate towards one or other end of the assertiveness scale or bounce between the two. There are very few at the centre, able to assert and get what they want, while accepting that the other person's needs are equally worthy of respect and consideration. The crucial difference between assertiveness and aggressiveness, and one that is often misunderstood, is that while being assertive communicates 'I'm going to stand up for what I need, and I will take your needs into consideration too', being aggressive communicates 'I'm going to stand up for what I need, and I don't give a damn about you.'

Of course, even when we get it right, asserting what we want doesn't guarantee a good result every time. It can be risky. People may not like what they hear; they may feel threatened or resentful — especially if we've always been meek and mild. Some men believe that women saying what they want, rather than wheedling to get their own way, is unfeminine.

*'Being assertive has caused a lot of friction in our house. I think Bert finds it a bit threatening. Consequently life is quite definitely not easier and I have asked myself on more than one occasion whether it is really worth it. Then at other times, when I am able to get my needs met, it all seems worthwhile. Although I do feel the balance of power has shifted somewhat inside the family, only yesterday Dot referred to her Daddy as the boss of the house so we still have some way to go!'*

*'When I'm playing squash, there may be several of us on the court. When a particular game finishes, someone says, "Who wants to play next?" and everybody hangs back and says, "Oh, I don't mind . . .", so I say "I'd like to play" and everyone else follows my lead. One of the men may turn round and say, "You're very assertive, aren't you?" like it was an insult. They don't mean it to be nice, but I take it as a compliment.'*

Being assertive does not necessarily mean always having to be on the offensive. There are times when we can happily go along with what our children want, just as we hope that at other times they will follow our wishes without comment or question. When we know how to express ourselves assertively, we have a choice — another way of reacting — that can lead us away from the conflict and aggression that have become so much a part of our lives.

## 'For people to take us as we want to be taken, they have to know us.'

Being assertive means, first and foremost, letting others know how we *feel*. Some people find it very hard to express how they are feeling, especially as talking about feelings is often judged selfish and self-indulgent. When people become parents this cultural embargo on feelings can become even more marked. Many parents think their children need protecting from 'negative' feelings, such as sorrow, fear or uncertainty.

*'Although I became very depressed after my marriage broke up, I never talked about it to John because I felt it would have a damaging effect on him. I thought, "These are his formative years and he's going to have this fundamental scar about living with a mother who's depressed." '*

In her heart, however, this mother knew that she was communicating her unhappiness anyway in those powerful unspoken ways explored in Chapter 3. Our experience in the groups is that when parents do let their children know how they are feeling, their children cope perfectly well with what they hear. This doesn't mean dumping all our fears and insecurities on our children, but letting them know about our feelings when those feelings affect the way we relate to them.

*'There was a time when I wouldn't have allowed myself to get upset in front of the children because I wouldn't have wanted to frighten them or for them to see me out of control. I would have always wanted them to think, "Mum's always in control", but the few times I have got very upset it hasn't seemed to affect them in a bad way. They don't think "Mum's a loony", they just understand how important that particular issue is to me.'*

Men often find it particularly hard to talk about their feelings.

*'My husband finds it very difficult to talk about himself and*

*the way he is feeling. When he feels upset, he gets tense inside and he doesn't like that feeling so he shies away from it. When he feels bad it is everybody's else fault rather than his.'*

True to form, this woman's son, Peter, not yet twelve, also gets uncomfortable when people express their feelings — especially his mother. 'He wasn't used to dealing with, or having to think about, the way I was feeling. To begin with, we had quite a few battles. But as time has gone on, it has got much better. He looks at himself more now and how he's feeling, whereas before he was quite happy blaming us whenever he felt bad.'

Letting our children know how we are feeling encourages them to be more open in their turn. When we say, 'I'm upset' or 'I felt hurt', they will start to talk about their own feelings — getting the message it's OK to feel certain ways.

---

## Sharing your feelings with your children

How open are you with your children? How much of what is going on inside do you share with them? Are you quite comfortable with your degree of openness or do you pretend to be other than you are because you believe that is what parents ought to be? Do you believe that certain things should be kept from your children or can you let your children know that you are feeling upset or frightened or lonely? Can you apologize and let your children know that you are wrong or have made a mistake?

---

Letting our children know how we are feeling invites them to see us as people with needs and feelings just like theirs.

*'I had planned to spend the afternoon alone with my son and I was really looking forward to it. But it turned out that he wasn't the least bit interested and spent the first twenty minutes trying to get a friend round. Normally, I would have said, "Oh, yes have a friend", but this time I said, "I've planned today around you. I really want to spend time with you. I think it's important. I'm upset that you want to go off with a friend when I want to spend the afternoon with you", and we had a much better afternoon for it. I'd explained how I felt and I think he felt pleased I wanted to spend time with him.'*

'Telling lies to our children is wrong.
Proving to them that lies are true is wrong.
Telling them that God's in his Heaven
and all's well with the world is wrong.
The young know what you mean. The young are people.
Tell them the difficulties can't be counted,
and let them see not only what will be,
but see with clarity these present times.
Say problems exist they must encounter,
sorrow hardens, hardship happens.

To hell with it. Who never knew
the price of happiness will not be happy.'
                              *(Yevtushenko)*

Letting our children know how how we feel helps them to help us and educates them to take our needs into acount in the future, maybe to the point of actually avoiding interfering with them in the first place.

*'Peter and I were walking home from school one day when he kicked a stone (regular habit) and hit a woman in front on the leg. I said to him, "When you kick stones and they hit people, I feel really embarrassed because of the effect it has on them." "OK," said Peter, "I'll try and remember in the future." It was great to have such a positive response and I must admit to being somewhat taken aback by it!'*

It stands to reason that the more open we are about our feelings, the more likely it is that we will have those feelings respected. Children are often simply too wrapped up in their own activities to spare a thought for our feelings. It can seem like they are wilfully trying to wind us up when, in fact, they're not even aware that they are putting us out. Often, if we actually bothered to tell them how we were feeling, they wouldn't be doing the things that wind us up anyway.

*'It was time to get Mark ready for bed and he was arguing and fooling around and I said, "I'm really tired, Mark, I can't argue with you" and he said, "Oh, well, I'll probably win then!" and I said,*

*"You probably will, but I need you to help me by getting ready for bed." I didn't say any more and then he said, "Well, I'll do two things for you, Mum. I'll get my pyjamas on and I'll clean my teeth, but don't ask me for anything else!" I said "Oh, thank you!" It was all I had wanted him to do, and he felt he was helping me.'*

*'Hetty was learning to drive in her father's car. One day we went off for a practice drive and she was going very very close to the car in front. I pointed it out and she kept saying, "I'm all right, I'm all right, don't get so uptight." Then I said, "Yes, you may be all right, but I feel nervous" and she slowed down straight away. I was pleasantly surprised. I hadn't accused her of driving badly or dangerously, I didn't even tell her to slow down. It worked!'*

Most of the time that we are not getting our needs met, we need help and co-operation because it's the other person's behaviour that is interfering with them; but first we need to let them know why what they are doing is a problem for us in such a way that it maximizes the chance of them changing what they are doing whilst minimizing the risk of them feeling bad, angry or defensive. Our experience in the parent support groups is that children are most likely to change their behaviour when we confront them in a way that doesn't put them down or criticize them.

---

## Confrontations

Think back over some of the recent times when you have confronted your children or your partner. How did they react? If they reacted in a resistant, rebellious or hurt way, ask yourself whether you could have confronted them differently to minimize the risk of resistance and hurt feelings.

---

Angry messages and blaming words don't just make the other person feel bad, they hide what we are feeling. Hiding what we feel is now so common in our culture it's almost universal. There are two main ways we do this. The first is by making general 'objective' statements that seem to speak for everyone — such as saying 'People ought to pay more respect to the furniture' when we really mean 'I don't like the way you are jumping up and down on *my* sofa'. Other examples might be:

- 'Big boys don't cry'
- 'We don't do that, do we?'
- 'It would help if you didn't make so much noise'
- 'We don't smoke in this house.'

The second even more common tactic is to turn the tables and place the blame on the other person. We call these blaming messages 'you-messages' because they make *you* the subject of the sentence, when it's really *I*. At their worst, you-messages can be utterly annihilating — 'You stupid, stupid child . . . I wish you'd never been born' — and at their least bad, almost guaranteed to provoke feelings of resistance and defensiveness. They include all the labels we've already looked at (Chapter 3) and a whole series of statements that most of us use everyday, such as . . .

- 'You're late again'
- 'You inconsiderate little boy'
- 'Why can't you think before you speak?'
- 'You're invading my privacy'

Communicating how *we are feeling*, rather than making a judgement about what *our children are doing*, keeps the doors of communication open and lessens the risk of defensiveness. Here are more honest equivalents of the statements in the last paragraph.

- 'I get upset when you are not on time for things'
- 'I feel fed up when you leave your toys all over the floor'
- 'I felt embarrassed when you called that woman a fat lady'
- 'I want to be left alone.'

Many parents find themselves amazed by the difference a simple change of pronoun can make. 'It really made a difference,' said one, 'to turn things round and own the way I was feeling, whether it was pain or pleasure, thoughts or feelings, and say, "*I* am feeling . . ."' It has made a tremendous difference to the reactions I get from my children.'

Children send you-messages just as often as adults do. But where children's you-messages come across as laughably childish — 'You made me fall over' — adults' are often expressed rather more subtly. Nevertheless they often represent an attempt either to shift the responsibility for how they feel or to hit back and retaliate.

*'When Heidi, my daughter, does something that hurts me my natural reaction is to be angry with her, but now I tell her that I'm hurt rather than hitting out and wanting to make her feel as bad as I do.'*

Sometimes, when we think we're

being straight and sending an I-message we may be sending a sneaky you-message, apparently owning the feeling but actually loading it with blame words and heavy insinuations.

- 'I feel upset when you behave like a little baby'
- 'I don't like the place left like a pig sty.'

Loaded words like 'always' and 'never' can also creep in very easily . . .

- 'I feel upset that you always come home later than you say you will'
- 'It hurts me that you never care enough to tell me about your day at school . . .'

Letting people know how we feel about what they are saying or doing, *while they are saying or doing it*, gives the best chance of bringing about change when it really matters. Invariably, however, this is also the riskiest time. It is not easy to let others know how we feel without getting swept up by the feelings themselves — becoming too upset to speak or so angry that we end up saying things we later regret. In these circumstances, having a simple formula can act like an anchor, keeping us on the level emotionally and helping prevent blame words and put-downs creeping in.

'It's hard to remember all the parts, and to get them all in, but having a formula helps me not to get swept away by anger or frustration or whatever. It takes the edge out of my voice, and the sting out of the situation.'

Our experience is that the most effective I-messages have four parts. First, they let the other know exactly *what* is bothering us and, second, *why* it's bothering us; third, they state *how* we feel about it and, lastly, they request *help* to put the situation to rights again. At the beginning, it can help to stick to:

'When you (behaviour) . . . I feel (emotion) . . . because (reason) . . . so please (help) . . .
Examples might be:

- 'When you interrupt my telephone calls I feel frustrated because I can't hear the other person so can you think of some other way of amusing your-self?'

- When you're much later home than you'd said you'd be I get worried because I fear some-thing may have happened to you so can we talk about

ways of changing this.'

- 'I've got a real problem with the way the washing-up gets left — I feel resentful that I'm expected to be the slave around here! I'd like you all to help make it different.'

## Behaviour (what it is they are doing that is a problem for you)

Hard as it is to believe, people often don't have the faintest idea that they are bothering us. This is hardly sur-prising if we shy away from telling them. It is too easy to think those we live with should mindread. 'If he really cared about me, he'd change', we say to ourselves, 'He wouldn't leave this clothes all over the place . . .'

Giving a clear description about what it is, precisely, that is interfer-ing with us getting our needs met, enables others to know exactly what we would like changed. De-scribing the unacceptable be-haviour rather than flinging labels also helps keep judgemental words out. 'When you leave your clothes all over the bathroom floor' is also much clearer than, 'You are so untidy . . .'

*'I found I had to think more care-fully about what I was saying. Describing the behaviour rather than labelling it with the first thing that came to mind some-how helped create a gap between my immediate reaction and the emotion that went along with it. It took the heat out.'*

Sometimes it may be necessary to give information in our descrip-tions, especially when we are challenging very young children:

- 'When you scribble on the wallpaper, I feel very annoyed because it spoils it. Scrap paper is for drawing on.'
- 'Water belongs in the bath, not all over the carpet which then gets all soggy and makes more work for me.'

## Feelings (how you feel about it)

Many people find saying how they feel is the hardest part of the I-message. If they have not been

accustomed to using feeling words it can be difficult to pick the right one or even to know how they are feeling. 'I'm like a child,' said one mother, 'I can't always name what's going on inside me, it's like learning a new vocabulary.'

One woman, an articulate and highly-educated university lecturer, who hadn't talked about her feelings for years, found herself at a complete loss for words when she started trying to express how she was feeling.

'I found "When you ... I feel ...

because" very useful initially in enabling me to express what I was feeling although at first I found myself saying "I feel ... I feel ..." and not being able to finish the sentence because I couldn't think of an appropriate word! But I have found with practice that my range of feeling words has increased. I don't seem to be so repetitive ... the words "embarrassed" and "inadequate" are fairly new to my vocabulary.'

## Expressing your feelings

Here is a list of 'feeling' words. Read through it, noticing the ones that are familiar and think about when and where you use them. Reading the list will help begin to enlarge your feeling word vocabulary.

| | | | |
|---|---|---|---|
| pleased | elated | glad | calm |
| uneasy | grieved | comfortable | silly |
| contented | satisfied | embarrassed | cautious |
| bored | hesitant | scared | fearful |
| surprised | confident | daring | eager |
| uncomfortable | confused | angry | anxious |
| lonely | tired | discontented | excited |
| warm | solemn | frustrated | stubborn |
| relieved | hopeful | serious | apathetic |
| proud | despairing | energetic | annoyed |
| flustered | cross | foolish | jealous |
| kind | miserable | stupid | tense |
| inadequate | shocked | troubled | relaxed |
| trapped | weepy | loving | wonderful |
| happy | peaceful | awkward | flat |

This woman helped herself by writing a list of feeling words and sticking them on her kitchen wall so she would quickly be able to pick the right name for the feeling she had. The list of 'feeling words' given here should help if you have the same problem.

When it comes to expressing feelings, starting sentences with 'I' is only a start. If you follow it with 'think' or 'feel that' it is likely you are expressing a thought, opinion, or a value, rather than a feeling: 'I feel that you are ignoring me' is an opinion; 'I feel rejected' a feeling.

## Reason (what it is about their behaviour that is a problem for you)

It's much easier for others to change what they are doing if they are given a reason. Too often parents don't give a reason. They bark out a command and expect their children to jump to it or the all too common autocratic reason that is not a reason at all — 'Because I say so!'

Children want to know why. Having a reason is very important to them. Yet they are rarely given much practical information about what is happening and why; they are only told the bits that the parent thinks will affect them. Parents complain that their children are forever asking 'Why?' They find it irritating and infuriating. Children find it irritating and infuriating never to be given a reason. When parents do start giving I-messages, they are often amazed at the difference a description of the actual effect can make. 'Oh, I didn't know', says the child in genuine astonishment and adjusts what he's doing accordingly.

*'The children seem much more amenable about tidying up and doing their bit around the house when we give them a reason for it and they can see what effect it has on us.'*

It's important, too, to keep the reason specific. This helps differentiate between needs and values. I-messages are a useful way of getting our needs acknowledged and met; they are not a recipe for imposing our values. What's the difference? If the behaviour is affecting us in a real and tangible way — it's putting us out by making more work for us or we get a headache as a result — it is interfering with our needs. If it simply offends us, or challenges our ideas of how things ought to be, it's likely that our values are being transgressed instead.

'When I first started practising I-messages there seemed to be all sorts of occasions to use them. My first one started out as "When you leave food on your plate, it upsets me to think about all that waste", but when I got to the part that explains what effect the behaviour has on me I realized that my visions of EEC butter mountains and wine lakes didn't really constitute a tangible reason. Trying to come up with a concrete effect has made me see that a lot of what I thought were problems are really non-starters, frequently left-over values that I'm not even sure I hold anymore.'

## Help (a request for help in solving your problem)

When our children are behaving in a way that we find unacceptable, we need their co-operation. Luckily, children are just as capable of helping us as we are of helping them. Yet, many of us write off our children's capacity to help. Sometimes we are reluctant even to communicate that we need help from our children. We are perfectly prepared to help — that's what parents are for — but to be helped? It seems the wrong way round.

Parents who felt that way and then started using I-messages have reported that they under-estimated both their children's desire, and their ability, to help. They are astonished by the creative solutions their children come up with once they aren't being steered towards the one their parents have arbitrarily selected, which may not be the best one anyway.

'I had a lot of problems getting Mark ready and dressed in time for school in the morning. I have a couple of children I take to school as well, so it's not only him that is late. In the end, I did say to him "Look, I get very upset when you aren't ready to go because we're keeping David and Billy waiting. What do you think we could do about it?" The idea he came up with was that he wanted his clothes up in his bedroom so he could get dressed as soon as he got up instead of coming downstairs for them. Since then he gets dressed the minute he gets up and he takes great pride in being ready early. It's his solution! He wants to be up and dressed before the others even arrive.'

We all have strong temptations to tell our children what to do, but leaving the solution aside is a vital part of the I-message. Just as it's important to give a child with a problem time to come up with his own solution, so leaving space for the child to think of the changes he might make to help us when *we* have the problem is a powerful way of encouraging concern for others and fostering initiative.

Children, like adults, don't much like being told what to do anyway — tending to resist words like 'must', 'should' and 'ought'.

*There was a layer of toys all over the floor. I was feeling really fed up about tidying them away and I'd already said a couple of times, very calm and reasonable, "I'd like you to tidy up" and they either said "No" or "OK, in a minute" and they just hadn't done it. And then I said, "I'm really fed up with having the living room covered in toys. It makes more work for me", and I knew I'd got it right, just saying how I felt without providing the solution and went away and did the washing up. And when I came back, the floor was clear.'*

Often an element of humour can completely transform a situation. Children prefer novelty over nagging. Notes in the shape of darts 'flown' into the middle of a game that needs putting away or another stuck onto the biscuit tin, saying 'These biscuits are for everyone to share', can have more impact than a barrage of blaming words. One mother in a group had a problem with her son who would always forget to bring his lunch box in to be cleaned when he came in from school. He would leave it around with old mouldy crusts and bits of food. She would nag him and then give up and clean it out herself. Then, he forgot to do it one Friday and it stayed uncleaned all half term. At the end of the week, his mother peeped in and saw fungus and mould and wrote a note on it, 'Please clean me. I stink!' She left it on his desk and he came downstairs rocking with laughter thinking it was very funny, but he got the

message and it hasn't been a problem since.

Children are also perfectly able to work out solutions between themselves once they know we'd like their help. One of the women in the groups would get home from her part-time job, frazzled and exhausted, to be jumped on by her two young children. For months she submitted to it, realizing that her children hadn't seen her all day and had just as strong a need to see her as she had for a bit of peace and quiet. Eventually, she decided to let them know how she felt. 'It's not one of you that makes it so bad,' she sighed, 'but when you both do it together.' The next day she came through the door and was steeling herself for the onslaught when they both came rushing up to her and skidded to a halt. 'All right,' said the five-year-old to his three-year-old brother, 'you go first.'

Giving children a chance to put the situation to rights allows them to see themselves as part of the solution as well as part of the problem and gives them a sense of their importance in the family. When children have good feelings about themselves, and their abilities, their self-esteem is enhanced and a bad situation can be transformed into a good experience for everybody.

Sam White likes his music up loud. Sometimes his Dad comes in to tell him to turn it down or to go upstairs. He gives an option but not the option to sort it out himself. His mother reacted differently: she asked Sam whether he could think of some way he could sort it out once and for all. His answer was to save up for a pair of earphones. 'I prefer to come up with my own ideas', said eleven-year-old Sam, 'Otherwise, it feels that they've just got their way and I'm not allowed any say. This way I feel we're all happy. I'm happy with the music because I can have it up as loud as I like and they're happy because they don't have to hear it any more.'

'The idea of matching what I said to how I felt, being congruent, was the big thing for me. Before, I'd always tried to be tolerant, patient, kind and understanding. Now if I'm upset or angry, I say so.'

Toni Lewis was watching her young son, Miles, jumping up and down on a trampoline with a friend. 'Suddenly he picked up a cup of popcorn and started eating it. I thought it was rather dangerous so I said to him, "Miles, when you bounce up and down and eat popcorn at the same time I get scared that the popcorn will get stuck in your throat", and he carried on laughing and jumping up and down and wouldn't get off. He thought it was a big game.'

Toni brought this story to the group as an example of an I-message that hadn't worked. With the group's help she decided it had failed because she hadn't adequately expressed her fear that he might choke: she didn't want to frighten her child. His reaction to such a mild request was 'Come on, I've been doing this for ten minutes. I haven't hurt myself. Of course , I'm not going to hurt myself.'

Toni was sending a mixed message, saying she was scared without in any way acting scared. Unlike some parents who tend to overdo the 'feeling' words under the misapprehension that they'll have more impact that way, others are frightened of coming on *too* strong. Their messages are so watered down, the children don't get the meaning. They voice a mild concern when, in reality, they are scared half to death, or they're pretending they're loving when they're actually seething inside, or they're trying to keep calm and yet they're inwardly really shaken up.

Children, who are more aware of mixed messages than adults, need both parts of the message to match. Given the relatively greater impact, especially to children, of what we 'tell' them with our tone of voice, gestures and so on, it's important that the spoken and unspoken parts of our I-message agree. We call this being 'congruent'. It means matching what we're feeling on the inside with what we're saying on the outside so that the messages we are sending are all lined up together: we're feeling angry, saying angry and acting angry.

*'When my daughter said she didn't want to go to Barcelona this year, I tried asking her why in a nice, quiet, reasonable, mature way, although inside, I realized afterwards, I was feeling angry and disappointed. But she stopped me, actually said "If you could only hear the way you are talking." When she said that, I felt cross that I was being loving and supportive and all those things. So I got angry. "You bloody well enjoyed it last year. Why the hell don't you want to go this time?" And it turned out that that was really what she wanted to hear. Before she felt that I was not really interested, didn't care much one way or the other whether she went or not.'*

# 'Every time I congratulate myself for handling a situation with my children without getting angry, I promptly get angry ten minutes later!'

Anger and intense irritation are familiar feelings for many parents, so much so that when they start sending I-messages, they find that the 'feeling' bit of the message is often an angry one: 'I'm angry that', 'I feel furious', 'that makes me cross'. They come to the group and ask why they are sending non-stop angry messages — can they really have so much anger inside? Many also feel ambivalent about expressing their anger. Is it right or wrong? Should they feel it or not feel it, let it out or hold it back? Some are familiar with the school of thought that teaches that anger is always better expressed than repressed, whilst others have been holding it in for years.

Repression is unhealthy. However, in our experience, free expression directed against another person isn't always helpful either. We may feel momentarily better for the release, but the person on the receiving end is unlikely to. They are likely to feel anger and resentment in their turn. It is important to be clear about the difference between 'clean anger' and 'dirty anger'. Anger is dirty when it judges, blames and attacks the person rather than what they are doing. Anger is clean when it is a non-blameful expression of our angry feelings about the effect of someone's behaviour on us.

Learning to express our anger cleanly as and when it occurs can prevent the build-up of those feelings to the point where we unleash them in a situation that doesn't warrant our fury. However, even a carefully expressed angry message can still feel like an attack and invite a defensive response. For the other person our confrontation may be the last straw, triggering them to release their pent-up feelings of anger and resentment in their turn.

Yet, on the other hand, it's necessary to express how we feel. Anger is a very powerful emotion, unparalleled as a motivating force and one that, if not expressed can tie us up in permanent knots. But it's important that we break out of the pattern of being enraged to such a point that we are no longer responsible for our actions and do things we later regret.

With insight, people often discover that anger is not really the problem. More often, it's a cover-up for deeper, more uncomfortable feelings. Yes, it's real enough — it breaks things, hits people, lashes out with vindictive, scathing words

— but it's just the tip of the emotional iceberg. There are usually other, even less comfortable, feelings underneath. It is often, especially for men, safer and easier to lash out and express our anger than it is to show how hurt, fearful or vulnerable we feel.

We have all seen mothers take their 'anger' out on a child when he runs out into the street in front of a car. They are not angry. They are frightened, shaking, yet they can't express the fear. Many parents feel OK about showing anger to their children, but not the feelings underneath it, so their children grow up learning that parents can be angry but not sad, fearful or lonely.

As with our children, so we're often not upset for the reasons we think. Underneath our anger, we're upset that someone hasn't paid their bill and we're overdrawn at the bank; we're frustrated that we haven't had enough sleep; we're disappointed and hurt that a friend has cancelled a lunch date for the third time in a row. The children demanding to be taken to a film or leaving their bikes in the drive is just the last straw. They are not the people we feel angry at, but we've bottled it up so long we can't take it any longer and dump the full force of our frustration on them.

*'I haven't stopped getting angry as a result of going to the group. I still do, often. But now when I've stopped expressing my anger, I say, "Ann, I'm sorry, what is behind the anger is ..." and go on to identify it — frustration or annoyance or I had a plan or preconception that she didn't fit in with. I try and explain as well as I can what is behind the anger and she likes that.'*

---

## Finding what's behind your anger

Think back to the last time you felt really angry: what else were you feeling? What had happened to provoke the anger? What sort of feeling preceded it ...?

The next time you feel furious, STOP, take a deep breath, let it out and ask yourself what you're *really* upset about. Give yourself the opportunity of finding a way to express the underlying feelings as well as the anger by catching them before you explode.

---

With time, most parents find themselves using angry messages less and less. They find other words that more accurately convey how they are feeling. They also find that if they can deal with their hurt, upset feelings before they reach boiling point, a great deal of needless hostility and unpleasantness can be avoided.

---

## Congruent anger

Do you know anyone who is able to be angry in a way that doesn't attack the other person? If you do know someone, how do you feel when they get angry? And how is this different?

---

I-messages needn't always be about problems. How often do we let our children know that we really love them or appreciate something they've done? Using I-messages helps to get round the problem of praise. Instead of saying 'What a good girl!' we can say, 'I love it when you clear up without my having to ask as it gives me more time to get on with the things I want to do.'

*'I had been having a rather heated discussion with my teenage daughter about men — she's in an anti-men phase — and we had both managed to avoid getting personal for all the heat. It ended or at least came to a close for now when she announced she was going out. I sat there and thought about how nice it was to be able to talk with her — so different from the relationship I had had with my parents. When she came downstairs again, my first "postive I-message" just popped out, something like "You know I really enjoy the way we can talk and you can hold your own in a debate like that — I know we don't always agree yet it gives me pleasure to know you think I'm worth arguing with." As she left she gave me one of the warmest hugs I'd had from her in ages.'*

We can also use I-messages pre-emptively, to forestall possible problems arising. Saying, 'I'm not feeling very good at the moment and I need some peace and quiet for myself' warns our children that we are in a fragile state and gives them a chance to adapt their behaviour. Giving children more information about the arrangements that concern them can also avoid potential conflicts. When they are told what will be happening in advance instead of being told to get ready to go out without being told where they are going or even consulted about it, they will often co-operate or at least let their feelings be known so that we can work out a mutually acceptable solution well ahead of time.

*'I used to travel quite a lot with my two sons after my marriage broke up. We'd go off and stay with friends. My children didn't like sitting in the car for any length of time, they'd get bored and restless. I found their arguing and fighting very distracting. I started trying to prevent this arising by getting together on Friday night, if we were going away on Saturday, and again first thing in the morning, and telling them who we were going to see and how long it would take. I'd say something like, "It would really help me if you had what you need to keep your-selves occupied for two hours because I cannot drive the car safely with you two complaining that you don't have enough to do, or fighting." It took some time for them to get the hang of it, but it made a big difference once they did.'*

## 'Clear them up yourself.'

It's unrealistic to suppose that we will get these copybook responses all of the time. I-messages carry no guarantee of success. A lot of the time our challenges may be met with resistance or seem to have no effect.

The most common reason why I-messages fail is that there is a con-flict of needs — we have a need for our child not to behave in a certain way and he has a need to carry on doing whatever he's involved with. In these cases, I-messages are only a prelude to the problem-solving steps outlined in the next chapter.

'My children love to slide down the bath slope at bathtime, which makes the water splash onto the carpet, and I have tried I-messages to no avail', said one mother. 'I have said, "All this water on the carpet is making me cross because it's ruin-ing it and I don't have the money to buy another one and, anyway, I don't like it all squelchy when I want to take my bath", and they just carry on laughing and splash-ing regardless.'

When she brought this example up in the group, this woman found that her I-messages weren't work-ing because the situation was inap-propriate. She needs to move on to the next chapter and negotiate so that the children get to have fun and she gets to have a dry carpet.

Even if our children don't have a

need that conflicts directly with our own, resistance is sometimes inevitable. No one *likes* to know that what they are doing is a problem for someone else. It is difficult to hear that our behaviour has led to someone feeling hurt or annoyed. However unblamefully we've phrased our challenge, our children might still respond aggressively or sullenly, go off in a huff, slam doors and refuse to discuss the matter, argue and fight back or burst into tears. Even when we've tried very hard not to blame them for how we are feeling, they might *feel* blamed. They might have problems of their own and being confronted with an apparently minor thing is just the last straw.

When we challenge our children and get angry, upset reactions in return, we have a choice about how we react. We can simply adapt our I-message and send it again: 'When you react defensively to me, it feels as though you aren't listening to a word that I say and I feel (volume rising) THOROUGHLY FRUST-RATED.' But this way we run the risk of triggering an even more defensive response so that we both get even more upset. They react, we confront them about reacting ('Don't talk to your Mother like that'), they react to the way we confront them and so on until a full-scale argument breaks out. It's an all too familiar scenario in many families.

An alternative way forward is by changing gear rather than taking up the gauntlet: alternating I-messages with reflective listening until the child's emotions are sufficiently calm for us to be able to repeat our original statement. Here's an example:

*Parent:* 'When you don't get home at the agreed time, I get angry because I'm frightened something may have happend to you.'
*Child:* 'Oh, for God's sake you're always fussing!'
*Parent: (taking a deep breath)* 'It sounds like you think I always worry about you unnecessarily.'
*Child:* 'Of course you do! You never accept that I can look after myself.'
*Parent:* 'You feel I don't give you any credit for taking care of yourself.'
*Child:* 'Especially not out at night' (calmer now).
*Parent:* 'I understand that you think I worry unnecessarily about you at night and you feel that is a reflection of my lack of confidence in your ability to look after yourself, *and at the same time* when you don't come home at the agreed time, I get worried thinking about all the mad people out there who could hurt you.'

Reflective listening resentment can work wonders. With practice, parents soon learn what works best with their particular child. For this mother, for example, it is letting her daughter's upset feelings be and then going back a little while later when the emotional temperature has dropped a few degrees.

*'Sometimes if she does get all uptight and storms into her room, I'll leave it for a while and then I'll go and sit next to her and I'll say "Do you want to talk?" and by then we'll have both calmed down and she will be wanting to talk about it and I will be ready to hear what she's got to say.'*

*'Louisa has a boyfriend who has been driving her about. When I discovered that he hadn't actually passed his driving test and that his Mother was allowing him to drive her car, I confronted her about this, expressing my anger at her boyfriend's Mother's irresponsibility and my fears for her safety.*

*'Nevertheless Louisa got cross and abusive and told me that it was none of my business. I was very calm. That amazed me! I just acknowledged her anger. I said, "You feel I'm interfering, that I have no right to pass comment on what you and Jonathan are doing. I appreciate that you really want to go in that car and you don't think I have the right to stop you doing it, and I'd like to point out to you that what he is doing is both illegal and dangerous and I'm frightened for your safety. And not only that, if he is in an accident and you are injured you will have no redress because he is not insured." Because I felt so strongly about it, and was able to be firm while acknowledging how she felt, she was prepared to acknowledge how I felt and it's not been a problem since. In fact, she's persuaded him to take lessons so he can take his test.'*

## 'If you tell the truth, you don't have to remember anything.' (Mark Twain)

In the groups, a question often arises about whether total honesty is always appropriate! Unfortunately, there are risks as well as rewards to telling the truth. Some schools of thought preach total openness and honesty: 'Tell the truth faster and have more fun per hour', one says, but the problem is that people are liable to come away, flushed with new resolve, and throw caution to the winds, offending others unnecessarily and not always acting in their own best interests. They stride into the office, Monday morning, 'Hey, boss, I've just learned how important it is to our relationship to tell the truth. You stink!', and the boss turns round, 'You're fired!' and they can't work out what on earth they did wrong.

In general, there is no doubt that telling others how we think and feel, will make life easier and more rewarding both for us and them. Yet we need to exercise a certain degree of caution in weighing up how far to go. It may feel good to get things off our chest, because that way we can be free to feel good about ourselves again, but how will the other person feel for hearing what we have to say? At times, it may be better to keep our message to ourselves or to find some other less risky way to help ourselves without hurting them.

Sometimes, however unpalatable our message, it is important to get it over. At such times, the real difference between being assertive and being aggressive will be apparent in our determination to help the other person cope with their reaction to what we have had to say. In this way we help ourselves and the other person at the same time.

Ultimately, our aim is to communicate in ways that increase our self-esteem and their self-esteem and benefit the relationship between us. If we know for sure that won't happen from confronting someone, we'll keep quiet; if we are sure it will be beneficial, we'll go right ahead; if we are unsure, we may decide to take the risk in order to add to the total level of honesty and openness in the world around us.

## Summary

- Our needs are *as* important as those of our children, neither more nor less.

- Our relationships with our children can suffer if we don't pay enough attention to our needs.

- There are three styles of paying attention to our needs and seeking to get them met.

  - **Submissiveness**, which rarely succeeds in getting anything met but is very common.

- **Aggressiveness**, which often works, but only at the expense of the needs of the other person.

- **Assertiveness**, which is rare and worth working towards because it is effective and helps us get our needs met while respecting the needs and values of the other person.

- To get our needs met, we have to make them known. This means using the personal pronoun, saying 'I' and owning our experiences without trying to offload them as 'You'.

- Having a formula helps us avoid blame words and put-downs, and increases the chances of our children co-operating to help us meet our needs.

- Confronting I-messages have four parts:
  - **What** the other is doing that is interfering with our needs
  - **How** that makes us feel
  - **Why** it is a problem for us
  - **Whether** the other person can think of a way of helping to resolve this

- I-messages won't always work, usually because we have a conflict of needs (see next chapter).

- Another reason is that, however hard we try to get it right and not to be blameful, our children may still feel resistant and defensive.

- All is not lost! Try changing tack. Reflective listen with those feelings until they get calmer and we can restate the I-message.

# CHAPTER 6

# NEGOTIATING AND HELPING EACH OTHER

'Somehow we always get into a muddle when all four of us try to be happy at the same time.'

Arguments, heated discussions, rows and fights are part of family life — at least every family that we've ever met — *however harmonious*. People living in the same house are bound to collide from time to time. While there are some practical ways of avoiding needless conflict, no skill, however expertly used, can guarantee a conflict-free life. Nor, perhaps, should it.

Many family therapists believe that a lot of problems in our relationships arise because we don't fight *often* enough, suppressing our feelings for the sake of an 'easy' life. The consequences of always giving in, never standing up for what we believe, are much more damaging in the long term, they suggest, than out-and-out arguments. Years of biting lips and clenching teeth can take their toll as problems that might once have

been swiftly and easily resolved build up beyond all proportion into unspoken grudges and long-lasting resentments.

In some families having good arguments is valued, and the most bitterly-fought disputes engaged in with no fear of upset feelings. In others, children are brought up fearful of breaking the calm, never daring to disagree.

In Judy's family, for example, arguments and fights were always strenuously avoided. Voices were never raised and no one dared argue for fear of being thought 'disagreeable'. It was rare enough to hear her parents differ over trivial matters — she never heard them actually *arguing* until she was about eighteen. 'My parents never, never argued and that set the seal on things. We weren't allowed to argue with our parents or with each other. Whenever I used to argue or fight with my sisters I would feel incredibly guilty for days afterwards.'

On the outside, life ran smoothly enough as everyone kowtowed to the family line. On the inside, Judy and her sisters became more and more inhibited about expressing what they were feeling. The price of such surface calm was increasing distance. Even as an adult, Judy couldn't bring herself to tell her parents anything that might upset them. She put off breaking the news of her own divorce for weeks. When she did tell them, they were, predictably, devastated.

Judy now realizes that her upbringing didn't equip her for dealing with the tougher problems of adult relationships and in a very real sense contributed to the breakdown of her marriage. She had no way of dealing with problems openly, straightforwardly; no practice at all at stating what she felt, listening to the other side and then working together towards a solution.

Many parents, like Judy's, fear that visible signs of conflict between them will somehow damage their offspring, when in fact they could provide a marvellous example for the future. If children could see and hear their parents openly disagreeing and then skilfully and successfully sorting their conflicts out, they would have a more realistic idea of how adult relationships operate.

## 'From the very first moment I put solid food in his mouth he spat it out!'

Unlike adults, young children have no fear of fighting. Many parents find themselves amazed at the violence of the scenes now daily taking place in what had always been a peaceful ordered existence prior to the arrival of children.

'Small children have no fear of violent confrontation: ordinary civilities are thrown to the winds as they rage, shout, howl, lash out and fight to have their own way', reflected the writer Fraser Harrison in *A Winter's Tale* (Collins, 1987.) 'The adult emerges from these clashes of will bruised and distraught, having endured an emotional battering that only the worst marital row could inflict; the child, meanwhile, shakes off the incident and is immediately her usual sunny self.'

It's these clashes of will that drive parents to behave in ways that in their more rational moments they probably wouldn't entertain — nagging, pleading, threatening, shouting, smacking. Though usually these accomplish little, parents often continue either for lack of anything else to do or believing that if they do it, louder, nastier and angrier, they will eventually succeed...

'If we tell Andrew and John at the last minute that we'll be going out, and there's going to be a baby-sitter, they are furious, but if we give them lots of warning they can have their fury before we've actually left so that going out of the door is not a problem.'

Some conflict inside the family is inevitable and important; needless conflict is just unnecessarily wearing. Making our needs known in advance gives the other person, or people, a chance to make their needs known in turn and can help avoid unnecessary conflict. When we let people know what we'll be doing or needing well ahead of time, we can then sort something out *before* emotions are aroused, everyone gets upset and the problem becomes a great big *issue*. The impact of these 'preventive' I-messages can be considerable:

• 'We're going to be visiting Granny this weekend and it would make a big difference if you could sort out what toys and books you would like to take so I can pack them up.'

• 'I'm going to be busy the whole morning today. We have an important meeting and I don't want to be disturbed. How can we plan the morning so that you've got everything you want, and I can be confident I won't be interrupted?'

• 'I'm going out this evening and want to make absolutely sure that we eat early so that I'm not late.'

• 'I'm feeling tired and want some time to myself so can you amuse yourselves this evening?'

Many parents postpone letting their children know what's going to be happening because they do not want to have to face their anger and upset before it's absolutely necessary. Yet advance notice gives the child time to make her needs and anxieties known, and the parent time to listen and help her work through her feelings.

*'My oldest daughter, Wendy, wouldn't leave my side until she was three-and-a-half. Just before that point, I had to go into hospital for one night. Swallowing hard, I told her about it a week before, dreading her reaction. She was very upset but we talked about it at various points all that next week, discussing what would be happening to me and how it was going to affect her, and by the time it was time for me to go she was helping me pack my case. And when she and my husband came in to see me whilst I was recovering in bed, she took one look at me and said "I want to go to playgroup"!'*

Simple changes in living arrangements can also cut out needless conflict. New parents get attuned very quickly to the hazards that lurk in every household and adapt their style of living accordingly. Pills and medicine are safely locked away in high cupboards, electric sockets are covered over, knives are placed well out of reach and safety pins left closed rather than open.

Sources of conflict, as well as danger, can also be avoided by making simple changes. If you don't like your child touching things on the table, move them out of reach; if your child is scribbling on the living room wall, provide something else for her to draw on; if she is enjoying tugging on the brand new pair of tights you set aside to wear, find her an old laddered pair to play with instead; if she wants to play with water, fill the kitchen sink and provide only plastic containers to play with.

Parents of very young children are very sensitive to the potential hazards lurking around every corner, yet when the time comes to make the home more accessible, rather than less, the instincts often do not work as well. Yet there are so many ways we can make life easier for ourselves *and* encourage our children towards greater independence, by modifying the living environment so it becomes more 'user-friendly'. Examples that have come up in the groups are: lowering the set of hooks in the hall so the kids can hang up their own coats after school; changing the height of the shower head so that they can reach it and shower themselves in the morning; lowering door handles and even light switches, or providing them with a safe small stool they can stand on; bringing scissors and glue and paints within their reach so that Mum doesn't have to be called every time they want to glue and stick and cut out.

## 'It's either scream and shout or give up.'

When our children are very young, we have to think laterally — on their behalf — to prevent accidents and avoid conflicts, but as they get older and we cease to be the caretakers of their every need, it is more helpful and much more time-saving to sort out problems *with* them.

This is not the scenario in most families, unfortunately, where conflicts are usually 'resolved' like boxing matches, with a 'winner' and a 'loser' and each side looking to score points at the other's expense. In some families, it's the parents who tend to lay down the law and the children who are forced into compliance. In others, it's the children who generally get what they want.

---

### Winners and losers

How were differences resolved in your family? Cast your mind back to your childhood and take a moment to remember. Was there always a 'winner' and a 'loser' — someone who succeeded in getting their needs met at the expense of the others? In what situations were you the 'winner' and/or the 'loser'? How did you feel in each situation? Bear in mind that there are many hidden influences on us as children that encourage this process, and no blame need be attached to those on top or underneath.

Most parents want their children to grow up willing and co-operative, responsible, thoughtful and tolerant of others. Ironically, the only way most of us think we can instil these qualities is by coercion, forcing our children to behave in ways that are less antisocial and more civilized. The thought of mutually negotiated solutions where the parent has to agree to co-operate as well as the child seems like a giving up of power. In fact, experience shows that parents have more *influence* if they do *not* use their power to enforce their solutions on their children.

Parents who use power to settle conflicts in the family often do so by attaching conditions. They 'buy' good behaviour with loud demanding orders and reinforce it with sweet manipulating words. They give treats when their children behave well and threaten when they behave badly. This system can work passably well when the children are very small and can be given a sweet to reward and have the television turned off to punish, but as the children grow and can buy their own sweets and maybe even have a television of their own upstairs, the parent tends to run out of power. The currency on which the relationship is built starts to be devalued.

Another potential problem with threats is that we risk being challenged to carry them out.

*'I can remember when my kids were little, it was as though one day I suddenly heard this stranger speaking, "If you don't do this I won't do that", "If you do this, then I'll let you do that." I was coming out with the most amazing threats and conditions and, even as I was coming out with them, realizing that I had no intention whatsoever of carrying them through. I would never remember to punish them as I said I would. As soon as I realized what I was doing I stopped, but I didn't have very much to replace it with.'*

It is the rare parent whose bluff is not finally called.

*'My teenage son and I were having a blazing row about his bunking off school and getting nowhere. Finally I just said "That's it — I've had enough, if you don't go to school this instant I'll drag you there." He slowly stood up from his chair by the kitchen table — all 5ft 8in of him (I'm 5ft 2in) and said calmly but lividly "How?"'*

## 'I'll cut the grass if you let me go to the cinema tonight.'

In some households, bribes and threats operate on both sides. Concessions are made as part of an ongoing bartering process.

*Parent:* 'I want you to cut the grass.'
*Child:* 'I'll cut the grass if you let me go to the cinema tonight.'
*Parent:* 'I'll let you go as long as you are home by 10 pm.'
*Child:* 'I'll be home by then if you give me money for the bus fare.'
*Parent:* 'I'll give you 50p for the bus as long as you do the washing-up.'
*Child*: 'I can't do the washing-up, I'm supposed to be cutting the grass.'

Bartered solutions never tend to be very satisfactory because so much has to be given up on the way. We may get what we wanted, or thought we wanted, at the outset, but the price can be high.

This is what happens so often in industrial 'negotiations', where everyone stands up and demands their rights — without so much as considering those of the other person. In this type of 'negotiation', a progressive trading of solutions often leaves both parties with rather less than they had before.

*Unions:* 'We want a wage increase.'
*Management:* 'You can have an extra five pounds a week as long as you increase your productivity.'

*Unions:* 'Well, we'll increase our productivity as long as we can have a shorter working week.'
*Management:* 'You can have a shorter working week as long as you sign a contract saying you'll never go out on strike. . .'

No wonder they have to go to arbitration so often! No wonder, too, that the whole performance has to be repeated before the ink is dry: all the problems and resentments are still there, seething underneath the apparent 'solution'. Similar half-settlements are struck daily in hundreds of thousands of households up and down the country by people who have been conditioned to see compromise as the ultimate virtue.

Compromise has been called 'Peace without joy or delight.' Of course, there are times when it can work wonderfully, but more often each side ends up feeling that they have got rather less than they wanted. Although compromise is one way of avoiding the win/lose trap of the parent *or* the child having it all her own way — halving the solution they first thought of is often not the best way forward either. There is another option, whereby parent and child join forces in the search for a solution that will satisfy them *both*.

Sounds wonderful but impossible say some parents when the idea is first put to them. 'How can *everyone* be happy?' Children, especially, accustomed to school with its emphasis on 'coming first' and 'winning', find this a strange idea. Surely someone *has* to lose? They can accept an either/or situation, they can't see how it could be a 'both'.

When they try it out, these families find that joining forces to find answers to common problems can work astonishingly well. Many parents, amazed by the results they get, say they cannot understand why they never tried it before. The truth is that many grown-ups are dismissive of children's contributions and ideas because of their 'immaturity'. They do not take their point of view seriously, much less stop to enquire what it is, although they frequently demand that their children step outside their own frame of reference and see things from the parent's point of view.

When we do take the trouble to take our children seriously, however, and give credence to their wishes and ideas, we may find we have seriously underestimated the potential value of their contribution.

*'I enjoyed Mike having his mates round to play football in the garden but was fed up when my plants got bashed about. One particularly bad day when they were on and off the flower bed all the time, I went out and confronted them. We all sat down and worked through what they could do so that they could go on playing and I wouldn't lose my precious plants. In the end the solution they came up with was a penalty point for every footprint on the bed and five for every broken stem! I don't think I have even seen such a careful — and skilful — bunch of footballers in my life.'*

This type of problem-solving calls for a mixture of the communication 'skills' we've looked at so far — expressing our own needs and feelings and then using reflective listening while the others air theirs, until we find the point where we can agree.

*Mother:* 'Jane, I'm unhappy about the way you leave the kitchen after you've made your sandwiches for school. We've talked about it before and it hasn't made any difference. I'd like us to sit down and talk it over properly.'
*Jane:* 'Not now Mum, I'm busy.'
*Mother:* 'You'd rather I didn't bother you right now?'
*Jane:* 'Yes, I'm trying to read, I'll make sure I tidy it up tomorrow.'
*Mother:* 'I hear you say you'll tidy it up tomorrow, and you've said that before. This is important to me. I object to having to tidy up after you, it uses up my time and makes me

feel like a slave, both of which I resent.'

*Jane:* 'Come on, Mum, I hardly make any mess at all.'

*Mother:* 'Sounds like you think I'm being unreasonable.'

*Jane:* 'You are! I'm rushed to get to school on time, the last thing I can think about is washing-up and tidying.'

*Mother:* 'OK, so you have a problem with time in the mornings and I have a problem with clearing up after you. Like I said, I think its time we worked out a way to solve the problem.'

*Jane:* 'All right, I'll talk!'

Having got to the point of agreeing to solve the problem, it's important to find out what the real conflict is before even considering solutions. One mother reported a recurring incident with her two sons who refused to wear yellow waterproof coats to school when it was raining. This particular family were over here for several years from New Zealand. Back home at their schools, everyone would have worn yellow coats.

*'After the parent support group session on problem-solving I sat down with them to try and sort it all out. By listening to their side of the story and digging behind the flat refusals, I discovered that they were laughed at for wearing their yellow coats. No one else at their school wore*

*anything quite like that. Here we were, arguing about coats when the real problem had been about not fitting in.*

*'I had never actually taken the time to find out why they were so much against those yellow coats, I was too busy trying to think of ways of forcing them to wear them.'*

It seems logical that when there is a problem between us and another adult person that we should work together to find a solution, yet it simply never occurs to many of us to involve our children in the problem-solving process. We may worry that including children in discussions of this kind will mean giving up some of our own authority or we may have become too accustomed to thinking 'for' our children, coming up with solutions and then enforcing them, to consider consulting them at some point along the line.

It's not just parents who are resistant, children too may be sceptical. 'When we suggested problem-solving', said one mother, 'my son said "what kind of new psychological technique have you learned now to let you get your own way?" ' Faced with this sort of reaction, we suggest that parents come clean about their motives and ask for help.

*'My first couple of attempts at getting any of the children to*

*talk things through were total flops. After one particularly fraught evening when not one of them showed up at the appointed time for supper I decided it was time to tell them exactly how I felt. I got quite emotional as I described how I had not been happy with the battles around the place. I admitted that I had not always behaved towards them as I would have wanted and was now really upset that they were not prepared to give me the benefit of the doubt as I struggled to find a new way. I pleaded with them to help. Problem-solving after that somehow just became a regular thing.'*

In families where the parents have got used to thinking up and imposing 'good' solutions, the children may resist the idea of problem-solving because they have got used to having solutions thought up for them. It's quite a challenge to have to start thinking for themselves after all this time, a bit too much like hard work!

'I find my children don't want to think up solutions,' said one parent who had always done it on their behalf. 'They say "I can't think of anything, you think of something." ' To such children, anything may seem preferable to having to make a contribution themselves. The responsibility's too daunting. 'Andrew's always afraid that if he makes a decision it will be the wrong one', said his mother 'and he'll wish he'd done the other thing. He *likes* having his mind made up for him.'

## 'Why bring that up now?'

Few people like conflict. It's easier to postpone it, to avoid it, to hope the problem will go away of its own accord. Children themselves may be reluctant to discuss problems, 'Why bring that up now?' 'Do we have to?' It takes an effort of will to get discussion going, to bring everyone to the negotiating table. Although there will be times when it's more practical to take a vote or issue an order, involving children in the problem-solving process can be a great time-saver — especially when it's used to solve those eternal family flare-ups like who gets to sit in the front seat of the car to go to school. At the beginning, laying down the law is quicker, but the time spent checking up to make sure the job gets done — punishing when it doesn't or setting new rules next week — can actually take much longer.

Nevertheless, some parents in their enthusiasm, overdo it. 'We tried to negotiate over everything for a while', said Judy Francis. It got to the stage where four-year-old Alison would put her hands over her ears and say *'No deals!'* So they let up on it for a while and since then Judy says that it's been much better. She has also noticed that although Alison still sometimes resists their problem-solving sessions, she is much readier to negotiate with her younger brother. 'If she wants something, and he says "No", she will make suggestions. "Let me play with it for five minutes and you can play with my Care Bear." '

While there's not going to be time to negotiate every aspect of family life, we give ourselves a good chance of solving difficult or recurrent problems by following the sequence outlined below — *especially when more than two people are involved.* It calls on the two basic skills covered in the previous chapters and — the fun bit — a brainstorming session at the end to see how many solutions everyone can come up with.

• Small problems can sometimes be solved on the spot in a mini-session. Larger problems often need more time — so establish a time and a place when you can get together to discuss the problem and find possible solutions — and make sure you are all agreed on when and where. Otherwise you may find yourself shelving it until the next crisis arises ... and the next ... and the next.

*'For the first six months we actually had regular meetings on the same evening each week where all the family issues were brought up. My friends were very sceptical — 'Family meetings! How American!' In fact they were great fun and very successful. They really got everyone into the habit of sitting down and talking things through. We seldom have to have them in this formal sense any more, yet regular problem-solving sessions are going on all the time.'*

There's no point even thinking about problem-solving if one or both of you are too upset to think straight. If you are calm enough, use all your listening skills to unflood the other's emotions. If you are feeling too emotional yourself, it can be helpful to say something like 'You've got a problem, so have I. Let's go away and think about it and get together again when we're calmer.' But set a time then and there, whether it's in half an hour or the following day.

• If trying this for the first time, start by explaining what you'll be doing and setting the groundrules: no one's going to lose; everyone's going to have the chance to have their say without interruption; everyone has to be happy with the solution. The first few times you ask them to negotiate, you may have to take time to acknowledge and talk through your children's scepticism. Many parents report that even the most resistant children become much more amenable once they have their doubts listened to and know that they are going to have a chance to have their say.

For children to have their point of view considered every bit as seriously as that of any adult's is immensely satisfying. Once they know their own point of view has been given full attention, they will be more able to consider the opposing point of view.

• Now agree on what issue you are dealing with — and stick with it. This may sound obvious, but some parents get so overwhelmed with the long agenda of issues awaiting solution they flit from one to the next, never satisfactorily solving any of them.

• Clarify what the *needs* are on each side. Conflicts arise between people because of clashes of needs. Unfortunately, however, the needs are frequently unclear and arguments develop over the *wants* instead. Here's an example that came up in one of the groups:

Ian *wants* his boys to go to bed at 7.30 pm — Grant and Alex *want* to stay up. They can fight forever about bedtimes, but what lies behind the *wants?* Ian helps the boys in turn identify what they need by asking 'What will that do for you?'

*Ian:* 'Alex, I hear you say you want to stay up later than 7.30 pm and I know that is important for you — I wonder what is important about staying up late for you?'
*Alex:* 'Well, I'll be able to play outside with Miles.'

When Ian asks Grant the same question the response is similar. When he asks the question of himself, his answer is to have time on his own away from the boys to write letters, read and do other things he's so easily distracted from during the day. Having discovered that the issue for the boys is about being free to stay up and do things with their friends and each other, and *not* having to be with their Dad, it was possible for them to negotiate a way for the boys to put themselves to bed when they stay up late, leaving Ian some free time.

It may take a lot of digging before the real need becomes apparent. One parent trying to resolve a sudden clash over her daughter not getting up on time to go to school went through many false starts: her daughter wanted to have a lazy time in the mornings so that when she got to school she didn't feel exhausted, so that she could concentrate on her work, so that she could do better in class, so that she would be ready for the big test coming up. It turned out that she was worried about the exams — her *need* was to feel confident about her exams whereas her *want* had been to laze in bed in the mornings!

• To establish what the needs are, let each person in turn say what they feel. Encourage the person who is speaking to state her point of view in terms of how she feels and what it means to her rather than blaming anyone else. Tease out the feelings and encourage them to be expressed as I-messages rather than 'You made me feel . . .' and, as the wants come up, gently challenge them with 'What will that do for you?' or 'What will that mean to you?', 'What is important about that for you?' and other variations.

• Where there are more than two people involved, it can be useful to ask the next person to paraphrase what the one before has said, to his satisfaction, before going on to state what the issue means to her. This ensures that everyone is listening to each other — and attempting to understand the issue from the other's point of view, reflecting it back until the other feels 'heard' and understood. This simple process can go a long way towards clarifying misunderstandings and does much to take the heat out of the situation. In general, the fewer people are at cross-purposes the more each is willing to consider the other's views and feelings.

One family does this by making the roles more formal. They have different hats. There's the Helper Hat and the Talker Hat. They throw a dice to see who starts and the person who has thrown the highest number puts on the Talker Hat. The person who is helping them find out what the problem is wears the Helper Hat. Then they swap. Formalizing the roles helps make the process less of a battle: instead of it being A versus B, it's A helping B, then B helping C.

If the emotional charge rises, as it inevitably will at times, it helps to deal with the emotions — gently breaking in, if necessary, to use reflective listening with the child rather than trying to continue at all costs. This will help move the process on towards a solution and save the whole session disintegrating into a mess of mutual recriminations — 'No, I didn'ts' and 'Yes, you dids.'

• Once everyone is clear about what all the needs are, it's time to move on and start thinking of ways of meeting them. The aim is to come up with as many ideas as possible. Have a large piece of paper and someone who can write quickly. Everyone contributes their ideas and they are *all* written down, no matter how weird or way-out. Giving vent to the most absurd ideas encourages freedom of mind and creativity and may actually lead to some ingenious solutions.

*'The children were having friends round to stay the night, and always before there had been arguments about the sleeping arrangements and who sleeps in whose room. So this time I got all the children together and explained what was happening and said "I want us all to think of ideas so everyone's happy with where they'll be sleeping" and they started thinking through the permutations and then my daughter said "We all sleep together!" and everyone laughed, but when we went through the list at the end, I thought "Why not?" so I said "If we put two big mattresses down in the big room and ask the others to bring sleeping bags would you be happy with that?" and they were.'*

Although a guiding hand may occasionally be necessary, it's best to be as unobtrusive as possible, especially when children start volunteering their solutions. Evaluating each solution as it goes into the melting pot, as is all too easy, will soon deter them from offering anything else. Saying 'That's ridiculous', 'That wouldn't work' or 'We can't afford *that*' risks the retort 'You never like anything we suggest, it's a waste of time'. Parents generally say they've found it best to be completely silent, allowing their child/ren to put forward his/their ideas before adding one or two of their own.

• Once all the ideas have been written down (without putting anyone's name next to the suggestions) read through the list, selecting the ones that most appeal and crossing out the ones that nobody likes. Again, it's best to make sure that you aren't the one doing all the selecting.

*'The very first time we tried it out, my husband and I sat down with our teenage daughter to talk over times to be home by. We all did fine up to and including a long list of possible solutions. I could tell that my husband had to bite his tongue at quite a few of the ideas she came up with and that, she seemed to throw in a few crazy suggestions just to goad him. When we came to evaluating the lists he couldn't restrain himself any longer — just got out his red pen and went through crossing out all the ones that were unacceptable to him. She blew up and*

*left in a huff shouting things like
"I knew it was all a con!"'*

Once this family managed to get
back round the table over another
issue, they adopted a system of
ticking the suggestions they could
all straightaway agree on and
crossing out the ones they all
straightaway rejected. When there
were none they could agree on,
they would then look carefully at
all the ones in between to see if
there was a way to modify them to
make them acceptable.

• Having found your solution or
made your short list, ask whether
everyone's prepared to stick to
what they suggest. Children are
often extraordinarily generous
with their solutions — coming up
with resolutions most adults
would find impossible to keep. 'I'll
only ever watch television for one
hour a week!', 'I'll always make my
bed before breakfast.' They might
mean it without reservation at the
time, but lack the experience to
visualize what it's actually going
to entail.

• Many people feel so good by the
end of the brainstorm that having
found the solution seems more
than enough. It isn't. Write it down
and then agree how you are going
to put it into action. It is very easy to
end up days or weeks later arguing
over who was supposed to make
the changes required. It's also a
good idea to check that everyone is
quite clear about their involvement
and not just 'going along with' the
solution because everyone else is
or it's time to bring the session to a
close and they'd rather be doing
something else.

*'I tried a problem-solving ses-
sion because of the amount of
junk food my son was eating.
Everything I cooked would be
greeted with a grimace and comments like, 'Yuk, what have we
got today?' So we sat and
problem-solved. We established
that his "need" was to have food
he liked and that mine was that
he would have food that was
healthy and good for him. We
came up with a few ideas and
finally we agreed that he would
eat what I put in front of him,
unless it was really totally detest-
able, without moans, if I dished up
fish fingers and chips twice a
week.*

*'It worked for a while and then
fizzled out. I kept to my side of it,
but Peter didn't stick to his. It
was a mistake not to have written it down. He started saying, "I
don't remember saying I was
going to eat whatever you gave
me."'*

Even when you don't have a formal
meeting, writing down the ideas as
they come up can help children
feel more involved in the process.

*'When Mary was about five, she*

*went through a stage of finding it really hard to get herself dressed and breakfasted in time for school. Every morning it would be, "Come on, look now, it's time to go" and the tempers would rise. Eventually I said, "OK, now, this is a problem for both of us and I wonder if you've got some ideas? Perhaps we can put our heads together and come up with something." I got out a pencil and paper. She couldn't even read at that point but I felt it was important to get all the suggestions down and for her to see that her ideas were important too.*

*'Mary's first solution was "Mary won't go to school at all." We both laughed but I wrote it down. I came up with a few, but the suggestion we adopted, and which she came up with, was "Mary would like to be first at the school playground in the mornings." I was amazed, but the very next day she got herself organized and we were down in the playground virtually the first and she was really pleased with herself. This went on for a few days and then it didn't bother her any more whether she was first or not, but by then she was in the pattern of getting ready.'*

Although it helps to formalize the problem-solving session, and many children enjoy the sense of a real grown-up 'meeting', it is important that everyone understands they are not going to be forced to comply with the solution if it proves unworkable. Having the freedom to renegotiate, is very important. Remembering that problems between people are usually about conflicts of needs, we need to keep an open mind and recognize that the solution may have to be changed as the needs change. If the 'solution' proves unworkable from the start, it will usually be because it was not meeting the real needs. At times like this, the negotiation process can usually be rerun, identifying

I BORROWED THIS FOR YOU FROM THE LIBRARY.

HOW TO BRING UP A GENIUS

the problem more accurately.

We would not suggest that this line of reasoning is any excuse for letting perfectly good agreements lapse. If, on review, the solution is still acceptable to everyone yet not being carried out, part of our role as parents is to help our children learn to honour a contract. One way to do this is to allow them to learn from the consequences of their actions — or lack of action.

The Yates family had an ongoing drama about all the lights being left on in the house at night when the parents were out. Although the children didn't think it was important, not setting the same store over the electricity bill, it was leading to such bad feeling that they decided to have a meeting. As a result the children agreed that on the nights when the parents were out it would be the responsibility of the last one to bed to turn the lights out.

'On the next evening that we went out, we got back and every *single* light was on. We couldn't believe it. So we walked upstairs and woke the children up and very calmly said, "You agreed to put the lights out and they are all on and we'd like you to stick by what you've agreed, so get up and switch the lights off and then you can go back to bed." They staggered downstairs, blurry-eyed, and switched the lights off. Although they complained like mad the next morning and all said they hadn't been the last to bed, they did take on a collective responsibility for it because the next time we went out, we came back and all the lights were switched off.'

## 'When we first tried problem-solving, we weren't sure if it would work. Now, we use the basic ideas in all sorts of ways.'

Brainstorming can generate as much laughter as creativity. Children love it once they get going and know their ideas are not going to be put down or dismissed. It can also be used for coming up with ideas as well as solutions — places to go, things to have for supper, how to tidy up quicker and easier, who to invite to tea on Sunday ... It's a marvellous skill for children to acquire — helping expand their imaginations and teaching that there are many solutions to problems, not just one.

Parents have also found brainstorming sessions useful for agreeing family rules, such as setting bedtimes and deciding who helps when with the washing-up or the housework. All families need limits and guidelines to live by. But in many families, the children have no say in deciding what these are.

Parents' desire for discipline is motivated by the best of intentions. They want their children to grow up reliable, responsible and well-mannered. They fear that if they don't set strict rules, their children will run riot and be generally uncontrollable.

The experiences of parents who involve their children in agreeing rules and limits, suggests that children are much more likely to keep to them than rules that have been arbitrarily laid down — especially the older ones. This was certainly the case for one family who decided to turn their spare bedroom into a schoolroom for homework and quiet projects.

*'It looked lovely, with their paintings and pieces of poetry up on the wall — everything they had done that they were proud of, but I could foresee certain things were going to happen. They'd play around with the computer, take food up there, leave the windows open ... I could see all the "don'ts" looming up and then, I thought, "No, it has got to come from them."*

*'So we sat down and I said, "Now the school room's all completed we need to think about how we are going to keep it. Schools run on rules. Perhaps we ought to have some for this room", and they said "Oh, yes, that's a good idea", and I said, "Well, let's brainstorm some ideas. See what you come up with, absolutely anything, and I'll sit here and write them all out."*

*'They came out with about thirty: no swearing, no throwing things, no banging. They had a great time. They thought it was hilarious. At the end of the session we went through the list, striking off any suggestions they thought they couldn't keep, "Because", as I pointed out, 'what we don't want is a broken rule. We want rules we can all stick to and live by", and they said, "Oh, yes, that's a good idea." So, gradually, the sillier ones got crossed off and we ended up with about a dozen — and, do you know, they were all the things I would have said myself. Except the last, rule number twelve, which was "No interfering by Adults"! I typed them all out for them and stuck them on the door and if anybody goes in there and starts interfering, usually me of course, it gets pointed out: remember rule number twelve!'*

Again and again, parents find to their surprise that when children are consulted, their opinions asked and contributions considered, they are more likely to co-operate.

*'We've got a small patch of garden we hadn't done anything with. I decided I was going to turn it into a cottage garden — you know, visions of poppies and delphiniums — so I said to Bobby, "Come on, lend a hand, pull out those two scraggly bushes", and Bobby said to me, "You can't. They're my goal posts."*

*'I was actually half-way through digging them up myself before it clicked what he had said, you know, that I couldn't turn his football pitch into a cottage garden, so I went back into the house and sat down and said, "What was that you said about your goal posts?" By that time he had gone back to reading his book, he'd given up on me.*

*'I asked him how he wanted his football pitch to be and he told me and then I explained what I wanted in the garden and we sort of planned it out together. And he said "Oh well, in that case I'll come and help you", and now we've got a football pitch with a cottage garden around the edges! And it's saved me a lot of trouble because I think he would have trampled my delphiniums to the ground, whereas now he's quite careful as he sees it as my bit of the garden.'*

As this example illustrates, negotiation does not have to be a formal round-the-table affair; it can be a quick exchange of viewpoints. Once comfortable with the principles involved, many families find that they conduct their meetings so informally neither side is aware of 'negotiating' any longer. As far as they are concerned they are just talking together and sorting things out between them.

As well as the immediate benefit of resolving conflicts on day-to-day problems, this approach encourages children to take more responsibility for themselves by thinking about limits and rules and how these should operate. It helps them become self-disciplined, less dependent on grown-ups to tell them how they should behave and conduct themselves, more able to distinguish right from wrong themselves.

The acquisition of self-discipline and self-control is a slow process and one that many adults never learn, let alone children. As Bruno Bettelheim points out in his book, *A Good Enough Parent* (Knopf/Thames and Hudson, 1987), it springs from self-esteem, having a good enough image of ourselves to act in ways that reinforce our self-respect:

'While criticism or fear of punishment may restrain us from doing wrong, it does not make us wish to do right. Disregarding this simple fact is the great error into which parents and educators fall when they rely on these negative means of correction. The only effective discipline is *self*-discipline, motivated by the inner desire to act meritoriously in order to do well in one's own eyes, according to one's own values, so that one may feel good about oneself — may "have a good conscience". It is based on values which we have internalized because we loved, admired, and wanted to emulate people who lived by them — for in this way we hope ourselves to be esteemed by these significant others.

'It is not much of a conscience which tells us not to do wrong because we might by punished. The effective conscience motivates us to do right because we know that otherwise we will suffer all the pain and depression of feeling bad about ourselves. In the last analysis, we will *reliably* do right only in order to prevent the pangs of conscience — to feel good about ourselves, not to avoid punishment.'

When children's behaviour is constantly being governed by others, they may see no need to learn to govern themselves since there is always someone else around to do it for them. Of course, our lives are all subject to a certain degree of control from without by means of our legal code, but within these limits we all find room to manoeuvre, to act responsibly or irresponsibly, well or badly, according to our own inclinations and the mental picture we have of ourselves.

---

### Looking at rules

Take a moment to think about the rules and limits that you had in your family when you were a child. Who set them? Was there any consultation? How did you feel about the rules and how they were made?

What rules do you have in your family now? Who sets them and how much consultation is involved in setting them? How do your children react to them? How do you feel about their reactions? Are the rules appropriate?

---

## 'You've got the car keys!'

*'Once I was having a very democratic argument with Jilly about where we were going to go and*

*Bobby was just sitting there and he said, "I don't know why you bother, you've got the car keys!"*

*There I was pretending to be democratic, putting on an act, when all the time I was the one in control because I was bigger. I had the car keys! Kids see through you like anything. But then I thought "Well I might have power, but they have power too", so I said to Bobby "Yes, but I'd like her to be happy about where we're going to go!" There was no way I wanted to spend my day with an unhappy child — and Jilly knew that just as well as I did.'*

There will be times in the life of even the most democratic family where it is not appropriate to negotiate. These times will vary from family to family, according to their values and priorities. The reality of family life is that parents *do* have more power than their children. The challenge is to use it wisely, exercising it as appropriate and always being awake to the possibility that the degree of power we exercise may need to be renegotiated as our children grow.

How much power we use depends on the level of freedom that we believe should operate within the family. This changes from family to family and changes, too, as the children grow older. How large our area of freedom is will depend on how far we are happy to share the power we have.

There is no right or wrong in this. People's values are bound to differ and there's no need for one to feel threatened by another having quite different limits. This can be quite a revelation to individuals who agonize about how far their standards and attitudes match — or veer away from — those of their family and friends.

*'It's OK to feel differently! My cousin has always protested about my allowing the children to travel by train on their own. She feels that they will be prey to all sorts of horrors. That isn't my worry at all. So in one respect I'm a very liberal parent. And yet she used to allow her children to take part in what seemed to me to be incredibly dangerous sports. They lived in Malaysia for three years and did the most amazing things — skindiving and harpooning fish — which I would feel most reluctant about letting my children do. I discovered it wasn't that one of us was more lax than the other. It was just that we attached different values to different dangers.'*

There are times when it simply isn't possible, or practical, to be democratic; when we feel it necessary to be firm and to stand by what we believe, 'No, I'm sorry, this matters too much to me. It's not even open to negotiation.'

When we know its 'No' we can avoid getting drawn into a row by saying it so calmly and firmly the child immediately senses there is no point in protesting. It is when we are hesitant or uncertain that children continue wheedling to get their own way. One mother discovered this for herself during one of her daily battles to change her youngest son's nappy.

*'Every time I'd change his nappy we'd have a screaming fight. Nothing I could do would calm him down. I reflective listened, "I know you don't like your nappy changed, I know it's horrible, but it's got to be done." But he'd still kick and scream. I tried an I-message, 'It makes me furious that you can't be still and calm for even a minute." but it had no impact on the problem either.'*

Then she realized she was always *asking* him whether he wanted his nappy changed, 'Kevin,' (her voice rising) 'Mummy change your nappy now?' when in fact she wasn't offering him any choice. When Kevin always said 'No' or indicated 'No' and she always did it regardless, he naturally protested.

*'So, I started saying, "Kevin, Mummy's going to change your nappy now" and the first couple of times he did fight and I said,*

*"OK go outside and have a good scream and come back when you are ready." And he did. It took a while but now we've cracked it.'*

Like so many of the useful lessons parents learn, the real insight came from the child; this woman learned another important lesson from her older son.

*'It was Mark who taught me how to be straight. We were playing a game together and he set it up and said "Do you want to be reds or blues?" and I said "Reds", and he said, "No, I want to be reds", and I said, "Well, you should just say to me 'I'm going to be reds, you're blues' if I haven't got a choice." So he said "Oh, yes, OK."*

*'A few days later we were coming back from school with two of his friends. It was freezing cold. After school we normally go to the shops for sweets but this time I said, "How about it if we go straight home and have whatever sweets are at home today?" And the kids all whined that they wanted to go to the shop. And Mark said, "Mum, you should just say that we're having sweets at home today if we haven't got a choice." Now we joke about it, I ask him to do something and I add " ... and that's an order, Mark!" '*

Some parents can tie themselves in knots in their efforts to be democratic when they know they are going to have to impose their own ideas regardless. Through the groups, they find that being clear in their own minds about what is open to negotiation and what is not enables them to be much clearer in their communication with their children.

*I'm very strict about sweets. Her health and teeth are too important to jeopardize by letting her guzzle whatever she wants. In the past, when I've told Alison she can't have sweets, I've felt guilty and torn — a nasty, autocratic parent. Now I can give her a firm 'No' and let that upset be, respecting it. I'm quite sure where I stand, but I can still notice her distress and acknowledge it.'*

Many parents find it helps keep the area of freedom open a little way by giving choices even when the point at issue is not negotiable:

- 'Would you like to do your piano practice now or after supper?'
- 'We are going out now. Would you like to put your coat on by yourself or do you want a bit of help?'
- 'I need time to myself after half past seven in the evenings. If you want me to read you a story, you must be in bed before then. If you want to stay up, that's fine, but I won't read you a story.'

Children respect firmness. Once they get a firm 'No', an absolute no, they hear it in the voice and respect it. This firm 'No' has nothing to do with volume; in fact, rather the opposite. In his book, *The Secret of Happy Children* (Bay Books, Australia, 1985), Steve Biddulph gives a great example of a technique he calls the 'soft-no' in action.

*'Jerrem is two-and-a-half and a handful. He seems to have learned infant-assertiveness, and makes demands over and over until something happens — whether it's to have ice-cream for tea, to interrupt Mum on the phone, or to get that shiny toy at the supermarket check out.*

*'His mother, Allie, is luckily discovering how to deal with all of this. Firstly she knows that this is a normal developmental stage for children of Jerrem's age, and that it won't last forever. Secondly, she had just mastered the 'soft-no' technique, and has become invincible!*

*'She sees other mothers struggle with their two-year-olds, and sees them caught up in rising tension: I wannit! No. I WANNIT! NO! I WANNIT, I WANNIT, I WANNIT! NO YOU CAN'T HAVE IT!*

*'The mothers become angry*

## How to put the soft-no into practice

The next time you find yourself in a situation where your child is demanding something, try the soft-no. Stay calm inside, keeping your needs clearly in the forefront of your mind, believing that your child will accept what you say. Be completely straight, do not offer explanations or try to justify your 'No'; instead, if your child gets loud and angry, try getting softer and quieter, even to the point of whispering.

*and tense and upset with themselves, assuming that they must match their infants red-faced loudness in order to win.*

*'Allie, however, does it differently. She simply says no, quite softly (knowing that children have excellent hearing). If Jerrem persists, she says it again, equally softly, at the same time relaxing her shoulders and softening her whole body (a trick which took a few hours to master). If Jerrem shouts, especially in a public place, she imagines herself carrying him bodily to the car, but at the same time softens and smiles inwardly. She controls her own feelings, rather than letting little Jerrem control them. The temptation to yell at him occasionally returns, but imagining the way he would enjoy this victory, soon removes this temptation.*

*'Allie is puzzled that just as she mastered the 'soft-no' skill,*

*Jerrem seems to have stopped his hassling.'*

The parents in our groups confirm that there is something extraordinarily powerful about this 'soft-no'. It's very difficult to argue against somebody who won't argue back, who, instead of getting louder and louder, just becomes very quiet and very still and just repeats 'No' in tones no louder than she did the first time.

To use this technique effectively, we have to feel calm and quiet on the inside. We sometimes suggest parents help themselves regain their calm by changing position; that they crouch down on one knee, for example, or sit down on the floor, take a few deep breaths and let them out before very quietly and softly telling their child that the answer is still 'No'. If we refuse to get drawn into the argument it's very difficult for there to be an argument. It takes two to tussle.

*I used to find it impossible to say 'No' quietly, but since I've managed to be absolutely clear in myself about what behaviour's acceptable and what isn't, I've* *found I can keep the volume down. He becomes very quiet, all his defences drop. I find it very effective.'*

# 'It's the fighting that gets me down, I know it's just going to get worse and worse.'

Penny, a secondary school teacher, once spent weeks struggling to keep two boys from fighting in school. 'It took a great deal of time and energy on my part, yet nothing that I said or did diminished their desire to fight. Eventually I let the fight happen, all the while worrying about getting the sack for allowing such behaviour to take place. They scuffed and rolled around on the floor, made attempts to punch each other. Finally, Kenny, the younger of the two, got his nose bloodied. Immediately the fight stopped and they were friends with each other. I couldn't believe it. The whole thing had only taken a couple of minutes and resolved everything and I had spent weeks trying to prevent it from happening.'

Even more than teachers, parents find themselves worn down by their children's fighting and squabbling. They can at least console themselves that arguments, an inevitable part of life in any family, can actually be healthy. According to a research survey carried out by psychologists Judy Dunn and Penny Munn at the University of Cambridge, when children fight and argue between themselves they learn to negotiate and to justify their arguments, skills that require a grasp of the feelings and wishes of the other child as well as a knowledge of basic social skills.

Their research, which was carried out on forty-three families in the Cambridge area, also showed that when parents tried to intervene, to bring peace and understanding, they would unwittingly intensify and prolong the struggle: 'Frequent interference by the mother resulted in more and longer-lasting quarrels'.

If parents can bring themselves to step right outside their children's arguments and leave them to them to sort out, the difference can be dramatic.

*'The other day, we were driving home in the car when Derek thumped his older brother, Keith. I didn't know what it was*

*about and I didn't try to find out. I just said, "Look, there must be some way of solving this so I am not sitting here having to deal with you fighting as well as driving, it's really upsetting me and it's dangerous. Please find some way of sorting yourselves out." Their solution was to go to each side of the car, as far away from each other as possible and look out of the window so that they didn't have anything to do with each other. It seems like nothing, but I can tell you it was magnificent just to have that bit of peace.'*

Of course, it is not always possible for parents to take themselves out of the argument. When there is a great difference in age and strength and one of the children is being hurt, it might be necessary to intervene, but on other occasions, letting the fisticuffs fly and giving up the thankless role of referee can be a big relief.

*'I used to intervene a lot when my daughters argued. They would always come to me, telling tales, "Jane's hit me", "Sarah's taken my toy". It was like a firework display all the time. So I resolved to stay right out of it. The next time they came to me, I sat down and said, "You know, from now on, these things are between the two of you. If you can't sort them out, you mustn't come to me. I really don't want to know!" and it has worked, to a large extent. They do tend to sort things out better.'*

In fact, it's worked so well that when this mother now attempts to step in and sort things out, she's told off: 'Stop interfering in our argument, you're always saying we've got to work it out ourselves!'

This principle of non-interference can also be useful when children come to us complaining that they are bored and don't know what to do with themselves.

*'I would wear myself out thinking things up for them, supplying ideas, arranging games and activities, getting other children over to play. I was always at their beck and call. Now I just reflective listen them, "It's hard, you just don't know what to do" and they sort themselves out.'*

## 'Don't speak to your mother like that!'

Many of the bitterest conflicts that arise in families, as in the world outside, are due to conflicts in values. Values are not needs, though they often come disguised as such in statements like: Children *need* ten hours sleep a night; children *need* discipline;

children *need* to look clean and presentable at all times; children *need* to pass exams in order to get on in the world ...

What's the difference between needs and values? Needs are specific — for food, warmth, shelter, company, love, encouragement. If they are not being met we are affected in a concrete and tangible way — we feel hungry or cold or soaked through. At their most extreme, needs can be matters of life and death: we can die of cold or fail to grow through lack of nourishment. Values, by contrast, are general and their infringement is not life-threatening. They may include not being made to feel embarrassed by the clothes our daughter wears or requiring her to say 'Please' and 'Thank you'.

Values are central to the way we live, important enough to affect almost every aspect of our lives. They underlie all our major assumptions about what's important — from how presentable our children look to whether getting their homework done is important or not. The beliefs we take on board without consciously knowing it seem to have the greatest power. We may encourage our children to think for themselves and yet complain when they 'answer back'; we may want them to grow up to be able to fend for themselves and yet refuse to let them out alone in the evenings; we may think we believe in equality between the sexes yet teach our girls to cook and our boys to repair the garden fence.

These beliefs, modelled for us by the adults in our own childhood, harden imperceptibly as we grow up, often starting to take on the status of 'truths'. We may not even think about them, or take the trouble to update them, but unthinkingly attempt to impose them on our children.

*'I was brought up a very strict Catholic and for years after my children were born I made them go to church just like I had done as a child. Then, when I was thirty-six, it dawned on me that I no longer believed in the Catholic religion and hadn't done for quite some time, yet I was still forcing my, by now, unwilling children to go every Sunday!'*

## What are your values?

Do the following exercise with as little thought as possible. Go down the list very quickly, putting the FIRST THING that comes

*(continued overleaf)*

into your head. While this is just for fun, it can show how strong some of your beliefs are without your even necessarily being aware of them.

- It is rude to . . .

  _____

- Children should . . .

  _____

- If you are good you will . . .

  _____

- Foreigners are . . .

  _____

- Women should never . . .

  _____

- A woman's work is . . .

  _____

- Being married means . . .

  _____

- If you eat what you like . . .

  _____

- Having green hair is . . .

  _____

- A good education is . . .

  _____

- Going on courses about parenting is . . .

  _____

The co-ordinators of our parent support groups do not attempt to preach a 'right' way to bring up children or seek to impose a certain set of values. To do so would be hypocritical since we make such a point of asking parents to respect their children's individual identities and points of view; accepting what they cannot change, allowing them to make their own decisions and loving them for who they are. We feel that the least we can do is to accept the different values parents may hold in return.

As our children grow and get exposed to influences outside the home, their values and opinions are bound to diverge from ours. The inability of parents to recognize their children as separate individuals, with their own lives to lead, can result in the breakdown in communication commonly blamed on the 'generation gap'.

Bob Geldof has exposed this brutally in his autobiography, *Is That It?* when he looks back on what it was like first hearing the Rolling Stones: 'That racket was the first thing I'd ever heard that felt like someone knew what it felt like. They were indecipherable to parents, there was no mutual point of contact but my father made the mistake of trying to appreciate the music. Appreciate! The whole point was that he couldn't ever, not even if he tried. Parents should never try to understand. I wanted something of my own. Something so totally mine, and incomprehensible to the older people, they could never take it from me, because they didn't know what it was. They only knew that it irritated them, but they weren't sure why. It wasn't just the music, it was because they couldn't get to me. When I listened to it, I was lost to them . . .' (Sidgwick & Jackson, 1986)

Debates about values are often the bitterest of all. It is as though to understand or accept someone else's values is somehow to lose our own. We become evangelistic, trying to convert others to our own way of thinking, *especially our children*, or defensive, jealously clutching our values to ourselves and shutting off from anything that conflicts with the views we hold.

In one family we know, the bitterest battles were about the need for a university education. Marie's grandparents had fought so hard to send her mother to college that college was seen as an absolute necessity for her — regardless of the fact that her inclinations and aptitudes lay in quite another direction. In another family, where the values were exactly the reverse, Danny was eventually disowned by his father for sticking his neck out and going to college rather than following along in his father's footsteps: 'If a trade was good enough for my Father and for me', said his Dad in exasperation, 'I don't see why it isn't good enough for you too!'

## Assessing your values

Identify a strong value or belief you hold (if it helps think of a running row you have with your children or partner) and ask yourself:

- What is it really about?
- Is it something that my parents felt strongly about?
- Is it something I got from rebelling against what my parents felt?
- When it is infringed, does it harm or interfere with anyone in a *tangible* way — can I see, hear or feel the harm that it's doing?
- Would a part of me secretly like to do it?
- What would happen if I didn't care so strongly about it?
- It is important to me that my children hold the same value?
- What would happen if I allowed them to believe differently?

Luckily, children are great at challenging our values! Indeed, it's often only when we have children of our own to bring up that we become aware of what our values really are. The advent of children in our lives demands not only that we make our minds up on all sorts of things we never thought twice about before — like food, clothing, noise, manners, education, violence on television — but that we also remain flexible enough to change our minds when our assumptions are proved wrong.

*'I came home from work one day to find that our three-year-old, Miles, had some friends round to tea. They were playing some game with cards. Eventually I joined their play, which was pretty unstructured, so I started trying to instill a sense of taking your turn to encourage more sociable behaviour — especially from Miles, who is very enthusiastic about games and always wants another turn quickly. The children seemed puzzled by what I was doing. Eventually I realized that the only person who was disturbed by him going out of turn was me. The other kids were perfectly happy. I had this adult concept of play-*

*ing cards, when you have your turn and then it's the next person's go, but as far as they were concerned they were just playing with pieces of paper.*

As a signed up member of CND, another parent naturally hated the idea of her son absorbing violent ideals. She tried to prevent him playing with guns and having violent heroes and hated the thought of him fighting. Then one day she went to collect him from school early and saw him having a fight with another boy in the playground and it was a revelation for her. 'You know', she said in amazement, 'it actually looked rather *fun*. I began to realize that all this talk about fighting that I had been getting so uptight about was part of a big game of prisoners and escape and make-believe and not nearly as terrible and sinister as I'd thought. Now I let him get on with it.'

Children often come up with unexpected ways of challenging our values. Ann Amersham came home from school and told her mother she had a Nigerian boyfriend. 'She was looking at me very intently to see how I reacted to this. So I said, "Oh, that's nice, tell me about him." And she said, "He's a very *black* Nigerian", and I said, "That's fine, are you expecting me to have a view that this is bad in some way?" I said, "I do have some prejudices. There are some

foreigners I wouldn't like you to marry because they seem to come from such chauvinistic cultures you would have an awful life. I'm much more concerned with you marrying someone who'd let you be equal, or more equal.'

The next thing Mary heard was that Ann had stopped having him as a boyfriend. 'Apparently, he'd been showing some prospective pupils around the school and was going from one classroom to the other, and she'd passed him. She said, "Hallo Emanuel" and he said, "Hallo Ann" and then as she went past she heard him say to these other people "That's my bit." So the next time she saw him, she said, "Sit down, Emanuel, you've got bad news coming" and she told him. I was really pleased that Ann felt she was worth more than that. "That's quite right", I told her, "don't you be anybody's bit." '

Even very young children can inadvertently challenge our values. One woman, looking after a vigorous little boy for a friend of hers, was constantly catching her breath as he hurtled around on some playground swings. She kept saying 'Watch out!' and 'Be careful' and finally admitted, 'I'm really scared when you race around on the concrete like that in case you fall down and hurt yourself' and he looked at her and said, 'So? I'm falling down and hurting myself all the time.'

As parents, we find our own values being challenged not only by our children but by other adults and parents who may not 'approve' of the way we're bringing them up.

*'Sam is a real climber and has been ever since he could walk. Every time we go to the park he is straight onto the climbing frame, right to the top, and stands there. People are always drawing my attention to it, saying, "Do you know he's up there?" when I'm right next door and would have to be blind not to see him or will actually say to him outright, "Get down from there, it's very unsafe", and I'll say "He's fine, don't worry, he's fine" and I find I'm suddenly defending my own values as well as his right to remain where he is.'*

## 'Don't do as I do, do as I say!'

We communicate our values, just as we communicate everything else, in spoken and unspoken ways. Like everything else, there are strong reasons for supposing that our unspoken values have the most impact.

'I realize that I want my little boy to be open and friendly towards the new people that he meets', said one mother, puzzled and upset because her son had started attacking strangers. Then it struck her that *she* hadn't got the attitude she wanted her son to adopt. 'I am actually withdrawn and wary about meeting people. What I want for him is at odds with how I'm being. Now I see that if I really want that for him there is more chance of it happening if I change the way I am and become more open.'

Life is so much easier and more peaceful when we can be sure that the way our children think falls in with our own view of the world. When they are little, children seem to take our values on board unquestioningly, but they soon come across the conflicting opinions of the outside world and start to waver and leave the shore.

*'At the moment our kids generally seem to accept our values, though at times when mine conflict with Dot's teachers she has to do some real soul-searching to see whose side she comes down on.'*

All parents have their own set of values and codes of priorities that they would like to pass on to their children. By their very nature, however, such values cannot be taught or instilled; they can only be presented as an *option*.

'Our style of life is to question things', says Alison Yates who has three teenagers living at home, 'and our children do this as well. When they were little it was easier, but the sort of questioning they do now challenges us at a much deeper level because they question the moral ideas that we hold and a lot of rule-making which seems important to us but we can't easily say why. The rules we had when they were little were much easier to justify and thus easier, probably, for them to accept.

The rules now spring more from our belief systems, values and life-style. Inevitably, I suppose, we came up against the problem of what time the two older girls came home in the evening. We kept stipulating times that were much earlier than they wanted and this became really quite difficult. They would ask "Why? What's the dif-ference? Why do we have to be home at one time rather than another time?" and I found that, if I stopped to think about it, I couldn't think of a good reason to justify why it was twelve and not two. It made no sense at all. If they were sitting around at home it wouldn't make the slightest difference to me whether they went to bed at 11.30 or 3.30.

'So, when we talked about it, I explained that it wasn't the time that concerned me but their safety. It seemed so obvious somehow but I'd never really stated it before, perhaps because I felt the time thing was easier to deal with than my fears about their safety. It turned out that the safety angle hadn't really struck them. They thought we were being arbitrary for the sake of it, or were worried about sex which wasn't the main concern. So then I had to ask myself, "Why is it safer to come home at twelve rather than two in the morning?" and the children convinced me that much later was often safer than relatively early because a lot of these things they go to — clubs and gigs and things — don't end before midnight. They pointed out that if they came home as early as we said they'd have to come home alone as their friends wouldn't be coming home until the event finished when all the kids would spill onto the pavement and the night buses would come at specific times to pick them up. I felt that there was greater safety in numbers than hours on the clock.

'Now I say, "What time will you be back?" We've talked about what's important to me, namely feeling that they are safe, and we've also talked about what that means — i.e., always being with a crowd and phoning us at any time if they need to. I've told them "I don't care what *time* you get home, it's *how* you get home that I care about. I want to know that you are safe." Because they understand my concern now, they are careful to get back when they say, to keep to those times. I think they have become responsible by being given responsibility.'

Sue, sixteen, confirmed 'Mum and Dad would always say, "You've got to be home at this time" and they'd give no reason why. So we had this deadline. I just thought, "Oh, they're being really strict, they don't want to wait up and be tired, or whatever." Then I'd get in the way of saying that I was staying the night with a friend so I wouldn't have to say anything. Now, because I've got that freedom, I'll make sure I come home when I say and that I don't come home on my own. I value it. I didn't like lying but I didn't know what else to do.'

Though we influence our children principally by what we do, obviously, we can also influence them by what we say. However, it's up to them whether or not they take these values on board. It's extremely difficult when we come up against issues that we feel very strongly, even passionately, about, but we cannot enforce our beliefs. We have to leave our children free to make their own minds up. All we can hope for is that they have enough self-esteem and belief in their own worth not to go along with whatever the peer group decides . . .

*'My parents tried every possible means to stop us from smoking: threats, bribes, punishments, all of which just drove us underground in rebellion. I didn't know how to approach this with my own children until working it through in the group. Then I went to the library, found all the medical articles I could about the effects of cigarettes, sat down and told them the facts as far as I knew them and my own feelings. I admitted that there was no point in my threatening them as they would just go out and smoke behind my back, so I wanted them to understand all the reasons for not smoking. If at the end of the day they really wanted to smoke there was nothing I could do about it, but I wanted them to start out really knowing what they were doing. I even shared with them how difficult it was for me to let them reach their own decision when I actually felt so strongly about it. My son is still wavering, but my daughter has even persuaded some of her friends to give up.'*

Common sense should tell us that children who trust their parents to be open, honest and non-coercive are more likely to ask for their opinion *and* to listen to it. If we already enjoy a relationship of mutual respect, built on openness and honesty, our children are more likely to listen to what we have to say. The irony, as too many parents discover too late, is that using power in a relationship to compel children to behave in a certain way will ultimately undermine their influence leading not just to rejection of the parent but often everything the parent stands for.

By the time our children get to sorting out values for themselves, our parental role has become more like that of a consultant than a teacher. This means waiting to be hired! It requires us to keep quiet until we are asked for our opinions, rather than jumping in and trying to impose them. It also means getting it quite clear in our own minds whether we are talking about values (beliefs, opinions, points of view) or facts. When talking about values, it's helpful to use I-messages — to make it clear that these are our own experiences, thoughts and feelings, not a prescription for the rest of the world.

Finally, like all the best consultants, we have to leave our clients free to make their own minds up. It may be a while — years or decades even — before they do. No one arrives at real, deep-seated values or beliefs overnight. The real effects of our work, love and care may not become apparent until our chldren are adults themselves with children of their own.

## When values can cause problems

One good way to discover the values that may be at the root of your family problems is to ask what you row about most often?

- Food?

- Cleanliness?

- Music?

- TV programmes?

- Punctuality?

- Friends that you think are bad influences?

- Styles of dress and appearance?

- Language?

And — just a thought — do they matter?

## 'Life is short, eat dessert first!'

*'Why on earth was I having running battles with my three-year-old about what order he was going to eat his food in? The ridiculousness of the whole situation suddenly hit me and I sat and laughed until tears rolled down my cheeks. With all the lovely things there were to do in the world, there we were having stand-up rows about whether you could eat strawberry jelly before baked beans on toast!'*

## Summary

- Conflict is inevitable in every family. What's more it's important: an essential part of learning how to live with others.

- When parents hide their conflicts from their children they deny them the chance of seeing them skilfully sorting their problems out and so deprive them of a valuable example for the future.

- Letting our needs be known in advance can help avoid needless conflict, as can simple adjustments in the house that allow children more independence as they are capable of taking it.

- Using our power as parents to settle conflicts has only the most limited effectiveness — threats and bribes soon lose their impact.

- Compromise is often not the best answer either because we all feel we have to give up something in order to arrive at a solution everyone can live with.

- Mutually-negotiated solutions that everyone feels happy with are rare but not impossible. They are usually reached through a combination of the skills discussed in the previous chapters, reflective listening and I-messages.

- Formal family meetings can also help, though it can be quite an effort to bring everyone together.

- Before we can look for answers, we need to establish what the problem is. Often fights develop over *wants* rather than *needs* and blind us to possible solutions that might be acceptable to everybody.

- When solutions are found, it's important to remain flexible enough to rethink them if they prove unworkable.

- The problem-solving technique can also be used to establish mutually acceptable limits in the home.

- Many children kick against discipline because they have no part in saying what the rules should be.

- Ultimately our aim is to encourage our children to become self-disciplined rather than imposing rules and regulations from above.

- There are times when even the most democratic parents have to take an autocratic line but there are still ways of doing this that respect the other's feelings and right to a different point of view.

- One of the most effective ways of saying 'No' is to say it as softly as we can rather than as loudly (the soft-no).

- Staying out of conflicts that children have between themselves can make life easier for us and be an important learning exercise for them.

- Some of the bitterest conflicts in life arise because of the different sets of values that we hold.

- The most effective way of influencing our children is by living our values not by preaching them or seeking to impose them.

# CHAPTER 7

# PRACTISING — INSIDE AND OUTSIDE THE FAMILY

'I wasn't aware what a slow process it would be. It's been much, much more gradual than I ever thought. To begin with, I thought I could do all this in no time at all. I had all the theory, and intellectually I agreed with it. I thought, "Well, all I've got to do now is to put it into practice", but, in fact, it's taken a long time for it to become automatic.'

If the idea of change is inspiring, the reality can be dispiriting. For every one of the parents in the groups, and for ourselves as well, change has come slowly, unevenly and, at times, painfully.

There are days when we seem to slide backwards, when we feel we've thrown it all away — when the stress levels rise, and tempers mount and our children come out with what feel like deliberately provocative and hurtful remarks. Then, we react impulsively, hitting out in the age-old way, matching their remarks with equally hurtful ones, letting our anger override our good intentions, hurling abuse, shouting, smacking, putting them down, calling them names and doing all the things we vowed we wouldn't *ever* do again.

For all the *'good'* times, when we remember what useful things we can say and our children react positively, copy-book style, there are *not* so good times when we find ourselves pushed way beyond the limits of our patience. When our children act in ways that hurt our feelings or embarrass us or hurt their younger brothers and sisters, we find it hard to be understanding and loving. Our own emotions of anger and frustration catapult us right back into the kind of behaviour that violates everything we most believe in.

Inevitably, as we lapse and relapse we will judge ourselves severely, being a hundred times more critical and condemning of our own efforts than we ever were of our children's. If we could be a little easier on ourselves, we would recognize that it takes more than a few short weeks to alter the patterns of a lifetime. We cannot hope to bring about longlasting once-and-for-all changes in family life; they come slowly, one step at a time.

At times like these, we would do well to practise some of our new-found principles of forbearance and acceptance on ourselves.

*'A lot of what I've learned is simply to get on with it. I'm more accepting of me. When things go wrong, instead of beating myself over the head I can say "OK, I did that wrong but I was tired/ grumpy/hungry/had a train to catch." The parent support group has really helped me to allow myself to be me and that in turn allows everyone else to be themselves as well.'*

'At first I used to get very annoyed with myself', said one woman, now one of our parent support group co-ordinators and running groups herself. 'Now I really don't mind. I've changed a lot. One of the people who was coming to my evening sessions said, "Tell me something. How can you guarantee that your four children will be out of the way and quiet when you do this evening session?" and I said, "I'm sorry, but I absolutely can't!" and, in fact, one of them did cry because she wanted to be in with me, but that was all handled. It wasn't a problem like it might have been a year ago when the whole of my evening would have been blown. I do think it is really important to get away from this idea of perfection. If you are always striving for something else you are never happy with what's actually happening.'

The ideas and alternatives people learn in the groups point out the direction in which they can move, but we always stress the risk of having too rigid a goal . . .

*'There isn't really such a thing as "failing". It's very easy to think you either do it well or not at all. Most of us do it a bit of the time, certainly not all of it. The more you are shown the direction in which to go, the more challenging it is.'*

As Bruno Bettelheim makes clear in his introduction to his book, *A Good Enough Parent* (Knopf/Thames & Hudson, 1987), perfection is not a human quality, nor even a desirable one: good enough *is* good enough.

'My title suggests that in order to raise a child well one ought not to try to be a perfect parent, as much as one should not expect one's child to be, or to become, a perfect individual. Perfection is not within the grasp of ordinary human beings. Efforts to attain it typically interfere with that lenient response to the imperfections of others, including those of one's child, which alone make good human relations possible.'

It seems that for every parent there is a 'learning stairway'. To begin with, enthusiasm for the new ideas is counterbalanced by the disheartening realization that we may not have been doing the best for our children.

*'When we looked at the risk responses, we realized that we were doing all these things, every single one. We looked through the list and we had done them all. They seemed to cover everything we'd ever heard any adult say to any child — not just ourselves, but what we were coming across every day with other parents, at school, in the playground.'*

The process of learning new ways is uncomfortable: once we know the way ahead, we are also aware of what we've been doing 'wrong' all these years. Before we were mostly muddling along, making do, dimly aware that there must be a better way somewhere. Now we know that there is a more useful way, we can no longer remain in blissful ignorance about the old ones. Suddenly, we realize that when we think we're listening *to* our children we're, in fact, talking *at* them, contradicting them or listening only half attentively to what they're telling us; that when we think we're constructively criticizing, we're actually putting them down; that when we try to bolster their confidence with lavish helpings of praise, we may well be doing just the opposite.

*'It was a major upsetting blow for me to realize that my way of responding was not serving people. That was awful for me, to discover in mid-life that so many well-intentioned and long-held beliefs were unhelpful. It left me feeling defenceless and incapable and lacking in confidence.'*

After the early enthusiasms, such realizations can be very discouraging. But they are the first stage towards change. Only when we are fully aware of the disadvantages of the old ways can we start to substitute them for something better; only when we realize the full impact of our actions and our words do we have any real motivation to change what we do and say.

Some of the 'new' ideas won't be all that new to us anyway; they probably echo many of those things we've always believed were important.

*'I found it very easy to listen and reflect what I was hearing. It's something I have wanted to do for years.'*

*'I've always felt uneasy about praise. It's almost like tying your kids to you. The groups have given me the confidence to go along with my instinct rather than what the culture decides.'*

Having alternative ways of behaving helps in the slow, hard path towards change; in fact our experience suggests it's essential. Even so the formulas can make us feel self-conscious. We wonder whether we will ever be able to be totally spontaneous with our children again. Will we always be working out what we're going to say next, biting our tongues lest a blameful phrase escape us, using learned responses that don't feel part of us?

Dr Thomas Gordon, who pioneered parent groups in the USA, has compared the process of change to 'Learning how to cut your meat left-handed when all your life you have held the knife in your right hand.' Just like learning to eat left-handed, using reflective listening, I-messages and descriptive alternatives to praise feels clumsy and awkward to begin with. Everyone wonders how long the unlearning will take; whether they'll ever arrive at a point where the learned alternative feels natural rather than stilted.

In our experience, every parent who perseveres will eventually master the skills, though the timing varies enormously. Some parents have mastered basic listening skills within a short while of attending our parent support groups, others need many months or even years of continuing support and encouragement after the end of the group to make it fully a part of their lives.

*'To start with, when I used some of the skills that I'd learned she'd say 'Oh, Mummy, you're doing it again!', but now they feel less strange to both of us. It's become a part of me and she's adjusted to it and I've become adjusted to the different reactions I get from her. When she accuses me of using a technique on her, I switch so it isn't so obvious. I've gradually learned how to use the skills in a way that feels natural. It's all to do with practise!'*

Learning new ways of communicating is like learning to do anything else — riding a bicycle, driving a car, using a typewriter. We can't expect to do it straight away. At first it is hard and feels strange, we make many mistakes, but this is all a part of the learning. We presevere and find that slowly, with practice, it gets easier until, after lots of practice, we don't have to think about *how* we do it, we just know.

Eventually, then, the responses that seemed so wooden and artificial just become a part of our natural way of responding. At this stage, where they are used entirely unconsciously without so much as a second thought, we have made it to the top of the learning stairway.

Many parents find that they are helped enormously towards change by their children.

*'We're learning a lot from Miles. He's supplied us with lots of insights, really showing us how our patterns are so ingrained. Really, in a way, he's teaching us how to bring him up.'*

*'Sometimes, when I think I'm being assertive, I'm actually being aggressive. I know because it produces a defensive reaction. Sandra says "Oh, don't be angry Mummy" or answers back or bursts into tears. I'm learning how I'm doing by the responses I'm getting.'*

*'I remember Jane saying "Thank-you for listening" after she had been telling me about some problems she had been having with her friends at school. She said "You know, Mum, I like the way you help me with my friends."'*

The feedback isn't always positive, however. Every parent of older children hears them at some point or another cruelly sum up their own feelings of failure and inadequacy: 'Huh, I don't know why you do your stupid course, you're just

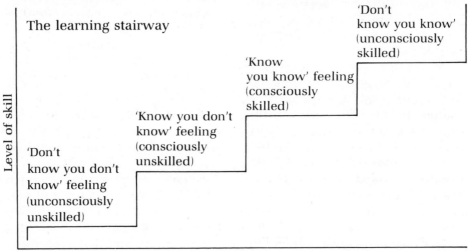

The learning stairway

Level of skill

'Don't know you don't know' feeling (unconsciously unskilled)

'Know you don't know' feeling (consciously unskilled)

'Know you know' feeling (consciously skilled)

'Don't know you know' (unconsciously skilled)

Time

the same as ever.' At these times, hard as it is, we need to remember that children are creatures of habit even as we adults are. If they have got used to us reacting in certain ways, they may find the new ones threatening.

Many parents report that, rather than reacting to this antagonism, swallowing hard and taking their children into their confidence often produces the best responses. Pointing out that the old ways aren't working for anyone, and asking for their children's help and support while they attempted to change for the better, can have surprisingly positive results.

*'When I first started practising*

*what I'd learnt, my two sons were very hostile, throwing in comments like, "Don't try that new stuff on me!" Eventually it got me down so much that I asked them to sit down and told them just how bad I felt. It was hard to do, but I told them I knew I had done things in the past that had made things difficult for us all and that now I was trying hard to find a better way and they weren't giving me a chance. They were stunned into silence as I came close to tears. It was as if I had really got through to them. They knew I meant what I was saying and the end result was that they agreed to give it a try.'*

'I learned so much so fast that I tried to shove it down his throat and it emerged that we had really big differences about the children and the way we were bringing them up.'

It's not just children we need on our side; it's best, too, to enlist the support of the other partner where we have one. Bringing up children is tough enough; it can be almost impossibly hard if the other half is openly sceptical or hostile to our efforts.

This is why we encourage couples either to join the groups together or, if childcare arrangements make that impractical, one after the other. It often turns out that these are the couples who make most headway because they are pooling their ideas and ideals rather than working one against the other. In this way they can operate out of a consistent attitude towards their children and each other. Of course, as we discussed in Chapter 3 this doesn't necessarily mean that their behaviour or their level of acceptance is always going to be the same; they are bound to find their own styles even within the new ways they will now have of being in the family.

Parents in couples who come to the groups without the other partner either being there or actively supporting their desire to change find that putting the new principles into practice does not necessarily make for an easier life. As one parent attempts to change and the other remains stuck in the 'unuseful' old ways, so old wounds can get reopened and new ones emerge.

'We don't have discussions any more', said one woman, reflecting. 'We only have arguments — and they start about half-way through the first sentence'. She would come back from the groups on Wednesday evenings, burning with evangelistic fervour, determined to change everything *right away*. She would see her husband calling the children names, being crushingly sarcastic and ordering them about and she'd rush in, hoping to salvage some shreds of their self-esteem before it was too late. She learned through hard experience that encouragement and silent example worked best. Criticism and interference simply got his back up.

*'Sometimes I feel the major conflict in parenting is between me and my husband, not me and the children. It really can be quite stressful. He and Christine were having an argument the other day and I said, "I'm not going to get involved, it's not my problem, that's for you and Christine to sort out." and he exploded. He said, "OK, that's fine, don't get involved!" Dick thinks that I shy away from confrontation. He feels it's not a question of whose problem it is. I should be backing him up. He's the grown-up, he's the parent. He doesn't think he should be treated on the same level as the children. It's demeaning, but I often feel that what the children are saying makes more sense than what he's saying but, if I accept that, he feels I'm betraying him.'*

To look at it from the point of view of the stay-at-home partner, it can be quite threatening to have all this new enthusiasm suddenly spilling out from some group or other. Many parents, fathers particularly, haven't given too much thought to the impact their day-to-day reactions have on their children and when these get questioned or criticized life can become very uncomfortable. We all like to change at our own rate, if at all, and not to be dragged along by other people. To have someone come along and say, 'It would be better if you changed how you talk to the 'kids' or 'I don't like the way you treat the children' is bound to raise the hackles.

When people coming to the groups run into these sorts of problems, we point out that it is, of course, just as possible to use the skills on partners as on children. Acknowledging the scepticism or the threatened feelings of the other half and backing off from applying too much pressure often helps enormously. Softly softly is the best policy here; the temptation to overdo the skills should be watched out for.

*'When I first used the skills, it drove him mad because it was so obvious I was just doing a thing I'd learned. He'd say, "Stop this rubbish, I don't need a psychiatrist." Now I listen, I notice, I don't need to say, "You're really tired, you've just come in from work." I act on that observation instead, giving him some time to himself instead of demanding he come and say hallo to the kids.'*

*'I knew that she wasn't going to like this new approach straight away. I am the sort of person who makes up his mind quickly and then jumps straight in ... But my wife takes months to chew things over in her own way. I don't see that as any better or worse — just different. So I decided I would just start doing things differently, talk about it whenever she seemed ready to discuss it and wait for her to deal with it in her own way.'*

For some people in the groups, the skills have had a very positive impact on their relationships with their partners. When she started using I-messages, June Hargreaves found they made a big difference not just to her relationship with her son but with her boyfriend. The old 'you' pattern was so strong, however, the I-messages took a while to master, but the breakthrough came one day when an argument was brewing ...

*'It was getting to crunch situation. Instead of pointing the finger and going "YOU, YOU, YOU ..." all the time I started saying "I", letting him know how I really felt, and we were able to continue to communicate. Usually our disagreements turn into major rows with both of us getting upset and shouting and storming out. This time he didn't feel I was getting at him, so he had nothing to lash out against. I wasn't throwing missiles which he had to defend himself against, or throw back. He could react differently because I was. It was a shock, though, for me to realize how often I blame others for the way I am feeling inside.'*

Women who tend to find it hard to be assertive out there in the wider world anyway, sometimes find it very difficult to start telling their husbands and partners what *they* want and need, especially if they've got into the pattern of going along with whatever their men decide. But even here changes can happen, as the following experience of a woman who had become recently divorced, illustrates.

*'I didn't have enough money for next month's food. I suddenly remembered that my husband owed me some money, so I rang up and told him that he owed me money and that I needed it. I couldn't bring myself to say I didn't have enough for next month's food, so I said "As you know I'm about to move house and I shall need it ..." But he sent me a cheque. Before, I wouldn't have rung up. I would have just, I don't know, probably have gone back to the bank manager and extended my overdraft. So that's quite easy, isn't it?'*

'Everything we talk about in the groups is just so much the opposite of what happens in school. My kids come home and say "the teacher was sarcastic" and whenever they stand up for themselves, they get flattened. They never get the responsibility for solving their own problems or directing themselves in their schoolwork.'

As we become more aware of the possible impact of what we say, we also become alerted to what we are hearing. Every day, teachers, friends, relations and even strangers relay messages to our children, and to their own, that are quite different to the ones we'd like them to be sending.

*'A very unhappy little boy was running up the road outside the school after his mother one morning. I stopped and reflective listened him:*

*"You seem really unhappy"*
*(sobbing)*
*"You don't want to go to school"*
*(shaking head)*
*"You'd rather be with Mum"*
*(nodding)*
*"You miss your Mum"*
*"Yes"*
*(more sobs)*

*After this he began to grow calmer. Unfortunately at that point, his Mother who had presumably been waiting round the corner came zooming up in the car and whisked him away saying how stroppy he's been lately and he'd better get into school or else and I was left standing there, feeling very upset . . .'*

Having changed our own way of thinking, it can be very hard to accept that other people are going to carry on unknowingly raising children whose self-esteem is crushed almost from the outset. We often have reports before the end of our groups from parents who walk out of supermarkets because they cannot stand the sight and sound of other parents shouting at their children. Others tell us that the new awareness can create bad feelings with friends and relatives. We are frequently asked what to do in such situations, how can you change people? On this question there is no easy answer: you cannot change people, only help them to change when they are ready. By relating differently to our children we may encourage a few others to reach that point. Nothing influences like example.

In the meantime, we have successfully sneaked in the odd exchange with a distraught child being trampled on by an adult relation: given a big smile and wink to the sullen toddler in a queue who has just been smacked by his mother; spoken a soft word or two to a screaming baby left in a pram or communicated an accepting 'bad luck' for the four-year-old who has just taken a tumble and been screamed at for dirtying his trousers. These are moments of bright light in a horizon of gloom, given in such a non-threatening way that mum, dad or granny may not even notice.

*'My sister's got two children, the eldest is five, and she's obviously never heard of our parent support group. She's always saying things like "You stupid boy, why didn't you do that properly?" or "You're so useless, why can't you be more like your younger brother?" and I can see him slowly being flattened, but she never seems to notice it. When I suggest trying another way, it just gets her back up so now I just put my penny's worth in, saying things like, "You must feel good about putting that model together" or just "You're a really great kid."'*

One woman, also a co-ordinator, has come to terms with the fact that it's not possible to intervene and step in when she sees children being unjustly treated by adults. 'It used to upset me no end. Now I console myself that I am trying to do something about it in my own

these skills is not so you can use them to manipulate or sweet-talk your child into doing what you want all the time. It's something you do *with* *your* *child* rather than to or at them.'

It's hard too to accept that the child we take such efforts to raise in a non-blaming, non-judgemental sort of way is going to be receiving all sorts of negative messages out there in the wider world. When everyone from grandparents and uncles and aunts to park keepers and policeman on the beat seems to treat our children in the old authoritarian ways, it can be very discouraging. We so want to build a new relationship with our child, it's hard to accept that some of our good work will get undone by the attitudes of other people.

Occasionally a parent questions whether the whole process is worthwhile. Their efforts seem like such a small drop in the ocean, can they really make a difference? And yet, with a little help and encouragement they can see that every little bit counts. Children, even from a very young age, are extraordinarily adaptable. They can soon learn to cope with one way of being at home and another way of being at school or at granny's. Giving them a regular taste at home of acceptance, trust and love can go a fair way towards compensating for the hostility of the world

little way. It might not affect that particular person, but there is another way and I am trying to pass it on to anyone who wants to know about it.'

Other parents may see us practising the new way and, totally misinterpreting what we are doing, be impressed for all the wrong reasons:

*People come up to me and say "You must show me how to do it, so I can get my children to do what I want", and I have to point out that the whole point about* they will sometimes find outside and also provides a great example for the future.

*'I was taking my seven-year-old to school and there was a mother at the school gate actually trying to push her child's hand back through the gate and saying, "If you don't get in there, I'm going to hit you." My son was really taken aback. He said, "Gosh, Mummy, that was a bit strict. Don't you think she could have thought of another way round?" and I practically fell through the pavement that he should come up with the idea that there could be other ways of dealing with it. That gave me hope. I now think that even for all the times I fail, perhaps the message will get through a bit faster to the next generation.'*

Most parents find that a certain relaxed realism seems to be the best policy when they find that their children are not being treated in a way they would consider fair and reasonable, together with the recognition that it's not possible, nor even desirable, for a parent to be able to control everything that goes on in his or her child's life. 'I can't change what's going on in school,' recognized one parent, 'but I *can* start making up for it, making sure that it isn't going on at home as well — building his self-esteem so he can deal with the hassles he's going to come up against outside.'

At the end of the day, we remind parents that relationships are like bank accounts. Every blow, every harsh word, every put-down or attack on the self-esteem is a withdrawal; every accepting response, every moment of listening, every cuddle and encouragement are deposits. We cannot guarantee that all our interactions or those of other people will be deposits, yet we can make up for the withdrawals we — and others — make with a deposit.

## 'I think it's very hard to do this in the context of one's own family, well I find it hard, but with other people it works much more easily.'

Choosing to change with the people we are closest to couldn't be a bigger challenge. The good news is that compared to practising these skills on our own families, using them outside with people with whom we are not emotionally involved is surprisingly easy: the emotional stakes are not nearly as high and old habits not as deeply entrenched. For this reason, we encourage parents to start practising on acquaintances, business colleagues, friends, relatives, teachers, shopkeepers, even parking wardens. This helps build their confidence: they invariably find that when there's less invested in the relationship, it's much easier to remain detached and come out with the most useful responses.

*'I find it very easy to reflective listen friends and colleagues, even passing acquaintances, because there is less emotional involvement. I have challenged a few people both in my parent support group and some of my kid's friends, mainly with success.'*

Practising on other people doesn't just provide a good training ground for the new skills, it can also help improve the quality of our lives outside the family. We soon find these skills can be applied *anywhere* and with *anybody*. They are not reserved for parents and children; they are about communicating with other human beings regardless of their age, status or relationship to us.

A surprisingly large number of people we come into contact with each day can benefit from a brief moment's listening. We have witnessed the lightness of a smile on the face of a harassed bus conductor or waitress whose hard day has been acknowledged. A few reflective listening responses can smooth the way between you and shop keepers, librarians or even the angry policeman about to take you to task for parking on a yellow line. Taking five minutes to use reflective listening to comfort the old lady who has fallen in the street will not only make her feel better at the time but may reduce the after-effects of shock.

Our new awareness of democracy, of power and powerlessness, can transform our relationships with people at work. One of our group co-ordinators is an exercise instructor. She says our parent support group has prompted her to change her methods of teaching completely: 'I don't tell anybody what to do anymore. Before I would stand there and say, "This is an aerobics class, here are twenty-seven exercises", now I just tune into what they tell me they need and we build the most appropriate work-out from there.'

Some of the men in the groups who are in positions of authority they have never questioned before, find themselves reconsidering their relationships with their colleagues both below and above. This is not always comfortable of course. For one, it meant putting himself on the line in no uncertain way: 'We have a system whereby all the team leaders in the firm hand in annual reports on their staff. It's a sort of yearly ritual; very gruelling for everybody, except for senior management of course who simply make out the reports. Well, I'd heard of one management team where the manager was reported on by his staff. I can remember at the time thinking I'd never have the confidence to do it, but I did and it was both devastating and useful.'

One schoolteacher, a deputy headmistress at a large London comprehensive, uses reflective listening with the children at school and has found it helps open up communication. 'When one of the kids has been thrown out of class, and is hanging around in the corridor, I just take three or four minutes giving that child a chance to talk. I ask him why does he think he's there, rather than leaping to conclusions myself, and invite him to focus on the problem. To begin with, there might be a lot of aggression or sullenness, "I'm always being picked on", but I just listen. Also I don't tell the child what to do, I say, "What do *you* think you could do?" and the child will often say, "Well, I could do this, or this" and most of the time will end up saying "Well, perhaps I'll go back to the classroom." It changes the whole situation, just talking it through.'

As professional people are gradually becoming more aware of the value of these approaches, and they lose the taint of newness, they are acquiring a sort of respectability. Even the hard core medical establishment is reviewing the way it deals with patients and taking some of these new values on board.

At the Walsgrave Hospital in Coventry, for example, a research project is now under way to assess the impact of reflective listening techniques on breast cancer patients, with half of the women being given half-an-hour's reflective listening the day before surgery and half simply invited to a traditional chat-type consultation. The team has found that simply reflecting feelings, particularly fears and anxieties, is having a real impact on how anxious and depressed patients become after surgery, with differences apparent not only immediately after the operation but for three months, a year, and even more. It's also beginning to emerge that the women being listened to reflectively are having fewer problems post-operatively with less need for pain relief and quicker and easier convalescences.

'Doctors are very good at thinking they are allaying anxiety by being reassuring, telling their patients not to worry, reassuring them about the safety of anaesthesia or the nature of the operation or their survival chances', said the surgeon in charge of the project, 'but in our experience often patients aren't reassured. We have found that saying, "Yes, I can hear you are very apprehensive about having an anaesthetic", or "You are concerned that you won't be around to see your children grow up", or "It's frightening to have something inside you that is spreading" has a more positive effect than any amount of reassuring words. Although these women are often in a very emotional state at the time, they later tell us how good it was to talk about their fears, and to explore them, and how grateful they were to us for listening.'

*'I was always a great one for solving everybody else's problems. For years I have been listening to other people, trying to sort out their problems and I'd get so overburdened. Now I listen and reflect people's problems and they feel good because they get it out of their system and I feel good because I am not getting a headache. I'm not taking on their problems. It's nice not to have to turn round and say "Go away — please — because I have so many problems of my own, I can't cope with yours as well."*

This mother discovered that not only was it much more effective to reflective listen her friends and leave them to sort out their own lives, but that it was easier on her. Coming up with solutions had always been a thankless task, whether she did it for her children or friends her own age. 'People used to ring me up and ask me what I thought they should do and I'd suggest something and they'd just go ahead and do their own thing anyway. That really used to frustrate me. I'd think, "Well I've spent all this time helping you and you haven't taken a blind bit of notice." '

It's not just on the everyday level that these skills are applicable. In times of real crisis, they really come into their own.

*'My sister-in-law nearly died on Christmas Day of a brain haemorrhage. I and a friend were with her and even when she was lying on the floor with convulsions, we used the reflective listening all the time. Everything she said we just reflected. "I feel so dreadful", "You feel so terrible", and in that extreme and desperate situation, it was totally the right thing to do. My sister-in-law's a difficult person at the best of times, very sharp, extremely intelligent. If she had felt we were mimicking her, she would have told us to shut up and stop repeating everything she was saying. As it was, I carried on reflecting everything she said for three days, all the time she was in hospital, just acknowledging how terrible she was feeling. When she got a little better, well enough to talk, she said how she had found my being there a real help, whereas the well-meaning friends who popped their heads around the door and said, "You don't know how lucky you are. I know people who had what you did and were completely paralysed", drove her crazy. She didn't feel lucky. She felt like death. It was a disaster for her.'*

Many people report that because reflective listening takes away that dreadful feeling of having to find something sympathetic or constructive to say, it frees them to concentrate on another person in a way that's entirely new to them.

*'My sister's husband had been made redundant. She was in a terrible state. My first feeling was "Oh goodness, I don't know what on earth to say" and then I thought, "I don't have to say anything" and that made it better. So I just put my full attention onto what she was saying and picked up on it. I knew that there was no point saying it was going to be all right because he was going to be out of work in an area where unemployment is high and competition is fierce. It wasn't going to be all right at all. But to say, "You are really anxious, it's a terrible thing to have happened" seemed to express an understanding of the trauma they were going through. It seemed to be what she needed to hear.'*

'Before I joined the group, I never ever went back to shops if anything was faulty. Once I learned how to be assertive without getting aggressive, I started trying it out. And it worked beautifully.'

People in the groups, women particularly, often find I-messages make an enormous impact on their lives. At last they have a structure within which it is safe to complain about shoddy goods or a bad car service, and to stand up for their rights without fear of becoming tearful or angry.

For working mothers especially, these skills prove useful, enabling them to get ahead and put themselves forward, stating what they feel and want without fear of infringing on the sensibilities of others or getting their male colleagues' backs up. It also enables them to get themselves taken seriously — important in a world where women are still not reaching the senior positions they are capable of, even though they often work harder and are better qualified than their male counterparts. 'They'd upset me and put me into a flap, so I'd react aggressively and hit out and lose my cool', said one senior executive, talking about how she would react in business meetings when she felt 'easy bait' for the male colleagues who pushed her around. 'Now I can confidently keep my head in most situations.'

Even outside the working environment, assertiveness skills certainly have their uses. Though many women say that they've felt so cowed by people in positions of authority for so long, this new freedom can take some getting used to.

*'I went to my local store and got something from the rack and went to pay for it. At the check-out, the girl said, "It's really £10.99, not £9.99", and rang it up. I said, "I understand you have to sell things at the price you mark them up and I feel short-changed." I was quite calm. I felt that they had made the mistake. It was their fault. I didn't even have to think out what I was going to say beforehand. And she accepted it and changed the till setting. Just like that! I left and stood outside for a minute or two and thought, "Wow!", feeling great and stunned at the same time.'*

Another woman always found that she would be both submissive and aggressive when things went wrong outside the home —

sheepish and easily deterred when she opened her mouth to complain and, later, aggressively furious with herself. 'I'd keep that aggression inside me and turn it back in on myself because I didn't dare go back and direct it at the person responsible.' Armed with I-messages, she challenged herself to take goods back to shops and found again and again that it worked beautifully.

*I feel very strong and very assertive. I can be clear about what I want. And get it. It works! Yesterday I took my car for a service at the garage and when my husband saw it, he noticed the aerial for the radio had broken off. I went back to the garage to sort it out, and said, "I feel upset because I brought my car in for a service and the aerial worked and now it doesn't. It's been broken off." And the garage man looked at me and said, "It didn't have anything to do with us." And I took a deep breath and said "But it happened here." And he said, "Well, we'll change it." And it was as easy as that.'*

Some people have a fear of saying what they want. They worry they will get carried away with all the strong emotions churning around inside them. With practice they find that the more they try saying what is on their minds right away, rather than storing it up and dwelling on the insult, the lower the emotional charge. Even so, using I-messages effectively does not have to mean remaining perfectly calm and composed if that's not how they're feeling. . .

*'After I got divorced I had to open a new bank account. Some days later I received a letter refusing me a cheque card. I'd been banking there for twelve years and they had records to see I was creditworthy. I was so furious, I went into the bank and asked why they had refused to give me a cheque card. They said it was because I already had another account and they were worried they'd be giving me too much credit. That really upset me. I asked to see the manager and, when he came through, I said, "You don't trust me" and then I thought, "No, that's not right" and turned it into an I-message. I was so upset and angry, I was shaking, but I managed to stay with how I was feeling. I just said, and kept on saying, "I feel very hurt and upset and angry that you don't feel you can trust me with a bank card when I've been a customer here for twelve years. I find it very insulting and it's making me angry. And I'd like you to give me a cheque card." After a short while, he apologized and said he saw no reason why I shouldn't*

*have a card and he'd get me one straight away. I was stunned.'*

This woman found that it was all right to be angry, to show her emotion, as long as she wasn't abusive or aggressive. In fact letting her bank manager see just how bad she felt about what had happened probably helped.

*'When I told him how upset I felt, he wanted to make me feel better. He didn't want me to feel bad, like I couldn't be trusted... Although I'd been upset, very upset, I hadn't been abusive, as I would have been before, yelling and screaming and being very rude and storming out and getting nowhere. This time I found I could turn my aggression into assertion by stating how I felt. And it turned out he really wanted to help me!'*

So often when we feel our rights are being infringed, the imaginary confrontation can build up out of all proportion in our minds. We feel got at and shabbily treated, although often the people 'responsible' simply have no idea that we're feeling that way. It's extraordinary the difference a little explanation can make. People are usually prepared to be reasonable once they know the impact their actions are having on us.

*'New people moved in next door and started doing the place up.*
*The noise of drilling and hammering was sending me mad. It got to the point where I hated them, really hated their guts, though I'd never even met them. I felt so invaded, so furious. I was in such a state about it that I didn't trust myself not to get carried away, so I worked out my I-message well in advance, "Sometimes the noise gets me down. I'm expecting a baby and I've already got one small child and I get tired. I'd like to know when you are going to be working on the house and how long the noise is going to be going on for."*
*'I rehearsed it a few times because I was afraid I'd get angry once I started talking. In the end I invited them up for a drink and let them know how I felt, that the worst thing was being so unprepared. I explained that I'd tense up when it started because I didn't know how long it was going to be going on for. It worked a treat. They explained that it was taking them much longer than they'd thought. It turned out it was a pain in the neck for them too! They said, "Yes, we understand, we should have come and talked to you first."*
*'Since then it's been fine. Now they let me know when they'll be working on the house and for how long. Sometimes just know-*

*ing what's happening, when it's starting and when it's stopping is enough. At other times, I might say, "I've got friends coming round by 9.00, so could you finish by then?" I still don't know them well but I feel quite different about them, much more positive. It's been very constructive! I can say, "I need forty-five minutes without noise now" and get it.'*

A lot of men find it hard to be truly assertive too. The role of disciplinarian and hirer/firer falls most often to men at work and yet there are not many effective models around to teach them how to handle awkward situations in a humanitarian way.

*'I had never been very good at confronting people about their performance because I was frightened of how they would react. I didn't want to cause too much of a scene and would be too lenient as a result. More than anything else I needed to learn how to cope with other people's upsets and anger.'*

The answer to this dilemma lies in the 'gear shifting' we looked at in Chapter 5. When we've challenged someone, even a complete stranger, about something we find unacceptable, reflective listening their angry, resistant reactions can be extraordinarily effective. Here is an example of an interchange that happened to a consultant we know who trains people in communications skills. He was flying home after a long working week away. He was very tired and longing to get home to his wife and family and had just settled into his seat to relax when he smelt smoke. At first he slumped further down into his seat hoping to avoid the smoke but it followed him down. Before long he felt thoroughly fed up, as much with himself as the man behind him as it made him feel inadequate and cowardly that he — as skilled as he was — wasn't doing anything about it. When the man lit up a second cigarette, he took a deep breath . . .

*Jack:* 'Excuse me, I've got a problem. I chose this seat because it is in the non-smoking part of the plane and I really can't stand cigarette smoke. I'm tired, I've had a long week and it's giving me a real problem.'
*Man:* 'Who the hell do you think you are? You own this f****** airline?'
*Jack (taking deep breath):* 'Wow, sounds as though you've had a terrible week as well . . .'
*Man:* 'Sure I have. They put me on the wrong flight and my secretary mucked up and I've already missed two appointments I should have made today . . . (continuing at length)'

*Jack:* 'Look, I understand that you've had a bad week too, *and* I don't like cigarette smoke because it makes it much more difficult for me to relax and I don't want to go home and take it out on my kids.'
*Man:* 'OK, look, I'm sorry, let's see if we can sort this one out . . .'

The upshot was that the smoker pressed his call-button and explained the situation to the air hostess who got him a seat at the back of the plane. Later, when they landed, the smoker was right behind Jack as he was collecting up his belongings. He stood back, a big 'be my guest' smile on his face, to let him out first.

Jack had spent many years teaching people how to communicate and teaching people how to teach people to communicate, and even he nearly balked at the prospect of having to assert his needs. As the example shows, doing so not only solved his immediate problem but also brought unexpected rewards, because, even in his firm determination to get across *his* needs, he was prepared to listen to those of the other man.

We, like Jack and every parent who joins one of our parent support groups, have much to learn and many old patterns to break out of. There is always more we can do to build both our own and our children's self-esteem. In persevering with our journey up the learning stair, who knows what further unexpected benefits we will uncover for us, our children and future generations.

## Summary

- Change is a long, slow process. This can be dispiriting and difficult at times.
- Especially those times when the pressure's on and feelings are running high, and we relapse into the bad old ways and nothing feels any different at all.
- It's important to be easy on ourselves, to recognize that aiming for once-and-for-all changes is unrealistic and only reinforces feelings of failure and inadequacy.
- There is no ultimate goal, no picture of perfect parenthood we should be striving towards, just a general direction in which the less useful things we do and say are replaced by more useful and effective ones.
- To begin with our responses are bound to feel stilted and wooden, particularly to our own over-critical ears. Gradually with practice, we will make them our own until we are using them automatically.

- In this context, the concept of a learning stair can be helpful. This takes us a step at a time, from the unconsciously unskilled stage of blissful ignorance, where we don't know what we are doing, wrong or right, to a stage where we are 'unconsciously skilled' and don't even know we are using a learned technique because we just do it.
- Children can sometimes be our greatest allies in our struggles to change, especially if we enlist their help and support.
- Ideally, for parents in a two-parent family, it helps if we make allies of our partners too but this isn't always possible ...
- In fact it's with our partners that the conflicts can be bitterest and the principles we've learned hardest to put into practice.
- There are also times when we can feel with our new-found awareness and insights that we're up against the whole world.
- Becoming more aware of the potential damage behind the most innocent-seeming remarks makes us much more sensitive to what we hear going on all around us; we all need the wisdom to accept what we cannot change.
- It's an uncomfortable thought that our children will be continually subjected to negative messages over which we don't have any control.
- Using the skills outside the family is an excellent practising ground and can help make our lives a lot easier and free of tension.
- Reflective-listening and sending I-messages tends to break through the unspoken, and often incorrect, assumptions we make about the attitudes and motives of others, helps clear away misunderstandings and enables us to go out for what we want. And to get it.

---

*Next steps*

Reading about getting on better with our children is a start. If you would like to learn more and put into practice the ways of relating to children described in this book, you might like to consider joining a Parent-Link group in your area or helping to start one near to you. If you aren't able to take an active part in The Parent Network at present, you can support our work by becoming a member.

For more information, please contact us at the following address:

The Parent Network, 44-46 Caversham Road, London NW5 2DS
Tel 01-485 8535 (Registered Charity No: 327136)

# INDEX